William Shakespeare

RICHARD III

edited by Jamie Lloyd

NICK HERN BOOKS

London

www.nickhernbooks.co.uk

A Nick Hern Book

This edition of *Richard III* first published in Great Britain in 2014 as a paperback original by Nick Hern Books Limited, The Glasshouse, 49a Goldhawk Road, London W12 8QP, in association with Jamie Lloyd Productions

This edition of *Richard III* copyright © 2014 Jamie Lloyd
Interview and Rehearsal Diary copyright © 2014 Jamie Lloyd Productions

Cover image: creativeXs

Designed and typeset by Nick Hern Books, London

Printed in the UK by CPI Group (UK) Ltd, Croydon CR0 4YY

A CIP catalogue record for this book is available from the British Library

ISBN 978 1 84842 426 5

Contents

Interview with Jamie Lloyd, director
Speaking to Richard Fitch

Why Richard III*?*

The hope is that every play in the Trafalgar Transformed season enters into a conversation beyond the theatre's walls. For theatre to remain urgent and apposite, it should at least chime with our times. *Richard III* is one of the most political of Shakespeare's plays and it feels as pertinent as ever. Not only that, but it speaks to multiple generations simultaneously, touching personal and familial concerns as well as the universal and the political.

If it speaks just as vividly now as it did when it was written, have you set it in its original environment?

At Trafalgar Transformed, we target first-time theatregoers through our £15 Mondays scheme. I'm sure many people would disagree with me, but, often, if you put actors in baggy tights and starched ruffs, it can alienate new audiences. Sometimes period productions can feel like they are of a completely alien world and, thus, the characters can be harder to identify with; they can hold younger audience members at arm's length. The play's imagined world of two rival factions and the machinations therein is absolutely at the core of our production, but we've created a more contemporary setting in order to make it more accessible.

You've set it in the 1970s, is that right?

It's fair to say that the actors on stage will look like they've just stepped out of the 1970s, but this isn't quite the seventies as we knew it. It is a dystopian vision, or rather an alternative British

history, that incorporates many other references that have
helped the actors to identify with their characters, from Le
Carré's *Tinker Tailor Soldier Spy*, to *Dear Leader* – Jang Jin-
sung's terrifying account of life in North Korea. In the 1970s,
Britain was scarred with political unrest, class warfare, social
and cultural instability and a secretively plotted military coup,
which is where our production begins. I didn't want to set it
arbitrarily in 2014 without a real reason for doing so. Things
would have to be taken to a crazy extreme for the events of the
play to happen on the streets of London today. However, for
many people, the 1970s felt apocalyptic. It felt like an
appropriately highly charged world that these characters could
inhabit, whilst feeling recognisably modern.

The springboard was some research I stumbled upon after I
joked to the designer that we should set it after the 1979 Winter
of Discontent (the name borrowed from the opening line of this
play, given to a particularly dismal period of social unrest).
Apparently, the aristocracy, fuelled by a fear of the spread of
Communism that was supposedly running rife in the trade
unions, planned to oust the Labour Prime Minister, Harold
Wilson. We imagine that such a coup has taken place after a
bloody civil war with Edward installed as the new military
leader, having killed Henry at the very beginning of the play. It
is a setting that allows for the faction-fighting of the play to be
keenly felt and creates an atmosphere of espionage and intrigue
that turns the heat up on the action.

*How has it been working with Martin Freeman and the cast he's
been leading?*

Martin is a phenomenal actor and he leads a cast of exceptional,
and exceptionally dedicated, actors. The rehearsal process has
been truly inspiring from start to finish. The cast was incredibly
forensic in the approach to the text without relinquishing a
sense of freedom or falling into the trap of 'singing' or
declaring the verse without a rooted, psychological
understanding of every single word.

The first thing I do with the actors is to paraphrase every line
into modern English in order to find the clearest, most

interesting and most useful understanding of the text. This leads to some very entertaining, colloquial interpretations, but it really helps the actors to make the text their own. It is amazing how so many words have several meanings and therefore how easy it is to decipher a line of Shakespeare, but not get to the crux of what the character concerned is *really* saying. One or two instances of those in any scene can warp the true meaning and the play can start to run away from you. The cast (even the children) were brilliantly committed to this exercise and I hope the narrative will be very clear because we took that time early on.

You have directed a huge variety of work. How does directing a Shakespeare differ from directing a musical or a new play?

The starting point for any text-based director is to form an imaginative response to the words on the page. I think this applies to any form. A musical may force you to be more technically strict – often an actor has to say a line within a fixed amount of music, for example; there are specific boundaries to adhere to, which can allow less time for jazz-style riffing with the text. I think that the actors who are really great at acting through song in a musical are often the best with classical verse, and vice versa. They are both heightened forms of expression and the formality of the language needs to be explored. There should be less distinction between actors who specialise in musical theatre and those who only do straight drama. That's why some members of our cast are actors from the musical world. A few of them have done little or no Shakespeare before, but have a natural instinct for verse-speaking because of their work in song. Ultimately, whether you're working on a musical, a new play or a classic, the main objective is to tell the writer's story in an engaging and dynamic way. As long as you tether every choice you make to the text, I don't see anything wrong with being brave and adventurous in the way you tell that story.

This play is famous for most – and sometimes all – of the deaths taking place offstage. Why have you chosen to give most of the deaths stage time?

I hope our production has a sense of simmering tension beneath the surface. I've often heard people say that there's no subtext in Shakespeare, which baffles me. In this play, most characters have a secret to hide and often there is a kind of volcanic emotion bubbling within them, which very rarely breaks out into a release. That creates an extraordinary tension. That's the mark of a great play – subtext; a play that is full of what is unsaid, unexpressed, or bottled up. There's a great emotional and psychological friction in that.

As part of our first Trafalgar Transformed season, I directed Alexi Kaye Campbell's *The Pride*, which is full of subtext. In the scenes that explore 1950s covert homosexuality, the characters very rarely announce what they are really thinking or feeling. We've tried to explore that kind of idea in this production of *Richard III*, which gives it a sort of hushed intensity, I hope; a bit like a spy drama full of secrets and lies. Having said that, to reach inside the disturbed and horrifying mind of Richard Gloucester, I think you need to see more of the terror he inflicts, hence bringing those deaths on stage.

The play is, ultimately, about life under a dictator, so the idea is to give the audience some sense of the extraordinary violence that these monsters inflict and allow that audience to connect, viscerally, to something unsettling. We couldn't do that without two key elements – the work of the best fight director in the country, Kate Waters, who approaches her work with great integrity, and the creators of the most authentic-looking fake blood – Pigs Might Fly. They both allow the violence in my productions to go to a whole new level of appropriate nastiness.

Would it be fair to say that many of your productions incorporate violence?

I don't set out to find plays that, first and foremost, require lots · of gore, but I suppose I do enjoy the challenge of making violence for the stage and, in particular, violence that seems just as graphic as the stuff we see regularly in TV shows, films and computer games. Audiences enjoy the thrill of it, but there is a seriousness in the exploration of this kind of cruelty. It is easy to objectify the real-life violence we see or hear about on the news. Deaths can so easily become, simply, cold statistics from a far-off land ravaged by war or scarred by a particular political regime. We hear about some terrible atrocity, then change the channel or make a cup of tea as if nothing has happened. We're immune to the personal loss and devastation; we don't feel the terror. The truth is that many people in other countries are living under a regime exactly like the one we see in this play. We have a duty to connect to that and confront audiences with that violence directly. I want audiences to have an immediate and raw response to that. The violence we create can often be very disturbing – but these are carefully choreographed stage fights using blood made out of sugar syrup. We're very privileged to be staging this violence rather than living through it in reality, but we can't forget that this kind of terror is faced by millions, in the real world, every single second. People don't realise how long it takes to strangle someone, or just how bloody a single flesh wound can be. I think it is important to take as long as it actually takes to do these deeds on stage and not cut them short, and when you really go for the truth of it, it can be simultaneously exciting and harrowing to watch.

Rehearsal Diary

Richard Fitch, associate director

Day 1 (Week 1)

Day one of rehearsals for *Richard III* shows no signs of us easing into the play. After a meet and greet which was sponsored by sunshine through the expansive Jerwood [rehearsal room] windows, and included the entire *Richard III* company and everyone from Jamie Lloyd Productions, Jamie and Soutra Gilmour [designer] unveiled the model box for the set of the production. They also spent some time explaining what Trafalgar Transformed actually means in relation to the space in Studio 1. What Soutra, Jamie et al have done with the old Whitehall Theatre is pretty remarkable. The stage floor has been raised by over two metres so where the performers' heads once were is now where their feet are. They've also extended the stage by four metres, meaning the audience will be closer than ever to all the action and now not just on one side of the stage, but two. 'It's a wide traverse stage but you have to treat it as if you're in the round,' says Jamie. Sightlines will be even more important than usual, then.

The space is not without its challenges too. In order to access some entrances, you have to negotiate ladders, steep stairways or by creeping through the sub-stage whilst other action is going on above your head. Possibly okay if one or two people are entering/exiting, but in a scene with the entire cast leaving at the same time, we may have to employ lots of our exit points in order to keep a sense of fluidity.

The set is a sort of dystopian version of a 1970s government building, partly inspired by the UN building. Rather than just setting it in a period without much thought, they've taken all that is useful from 1970s Britain, both politically and socio-culturally in order to contextualise Shakespeare in a more accessible modern setting.

During the presentation, Jamie speaks a lot of the secret plot to overthrow Harold Wilson's Labour government in the mid-seventies, which has since been heavily documented and discounted by government authorities. It very nearly happened, it seems, with drills at Heathrow Airport. 'My father was in the Territorial Army, was telephoned and was told by an anonymous voice to stand by for a coup. Then he never heard anything else,' Maggie Steed [Queen Margaret] pipes up. Something about the way everyone present is listening to Jamie and Soutra tells me that we have a cast of actors that will dive head-first into this idea of espionage, secrecy and the 'devilish plots' that Gloucester speaks of so early on in the play.

Day 10 (Week 2)

'That was my first ever drowning,' says Kombat Kate Waters [Fight Director] after an epic morning rehearsing one of the longest scenes in Jamie's version of *Richard III*, which finished with an equally epic fight sequence. Though it's a scene of considerable length, it's pretty straightforward in terms of its dramatic arc. Though I'm starting to realise that every scene (and, indeed, every element of every scene) in this production is even more complex than I originally thought. In characters like Catesby and Tyrell we are witnessing a distillation of several characters in one person, so the psychological shifts that these actors have to make are extreme and often sudden. In order to keep that sense of freedom while we all get our heads around everyone's thoughts from line to line, Jamie is keeping the staging fluid in all scenes, but it's particularly useful in scenes like this, as Kate likes her fights to come from the previous action. Nothing should feel manufactured in order to make a prettier fight. If anything, the combat in this show is all but pleasant on the eyes.

Along with the core idea that Jamie has about beginning with opposing political ideologies that become more tribal and visceral, I'm realising that the fights in this play will help transition the piece from being political and simmering to being tribal and volcanic, showing us what an ugly political world we've entered into, where we see just how dirty these characters can play.

With lots of battles comes weaponry and other details that we want to get right. We brought in military dress and arms experts to ensure that what the actors will wear and hold in the face of victory (or defeat) is as close as possible to what they would have worn/held in a 1970s war. There is a big challenge that comes with dealing with a Shakespeare in the twenty-first century where we could just text somebody in place of having a messenger enter to deliver news or shoot someone in the head instead of have a gruelling sword fight. Loosely placing our version in the seventies takes care of the phone issue – that and the fact that Jamie has conflated all of those characters that are only in the original for a few lines in order deliver news. But the gun challenge exists and becomes a question of logic. Kombat Kate is absolutely right to ask 'Why would they fight with fists if they could just shoot each other?' That's why disarming certain characters of their weapons is being created with just as much attention and focus as the rest of the fights, or indeed, the rest of the play. It's clear that along with contextualising every single moment comes the necessity to *believe* every single moment, both what is said and what is said with action.

Day 14 (Week 3)

After spending the first two weeks going through the entire play on its feet, we find ourselves, the entire *Richard III* company, reuniting in the rehearsal room (that is still sponsored by sunshine) to read through the play from start to finish… for the first time! In truth, it does make me think how much time could be wasted in hundreds of rehearsal rooms daily with initial readthroughs. I'm sure it sometimes has its benefits, but particularly with a Shakespeare it's *got* to be worth touching each scene at least once to break it apart a little.

Doing this certainly paid off for us. Even as we sit around our UN-like tables on the rehearsal set, the play is so much clearer to me. I really don't think this is because I have a physical version of everything in my head, because 99.9% of the blocking is still up for grabs (as demonstrated by my script, which has about eight versions of staging for each scene!), but I think it's due to the actors and Jamie paraphrasing each scene word for word. This wasn't just about 'achieving a translation of Shakespeare,' it was about deciphering Shakespeare's true meaning behind every word. These meanings often gave us options that spanned the whole spectrum from completely unhelpful to clear-as-a-bell perfect. Several versions of the text were used and sifted through in order find different footnotes and text variations. We also changed the odd word to make it clearer. It doesn't matter how good anyone is, no one will ever convince a first-time theatregoer that 'cousin' can be used to address several different relatives in a family. Why wouldn't you make it as clear as possible to the audience and use 'grandson' or 'nephew' in its place?

Also helping with the endeavor of clarity is voice and text expert, Barbara Houseman. By this point in the process, most of the cast have had at least an initial session with Barbara, which built on the session she gave to the entire cast on day one. We are also well into costume fittings and everyone has had hair and wig discussions. The play is shaped in a way where plenty of the actors get enough time to nip out for voice sessions or fittings, but Jamie is keen to flesh out our world so that it has depth from the very beginning by plotting in extra characters throughout.

After lunch, we began working through the play from the beginning again. Jamie had this idea to start the play with most of the cast on stage as if a bloody civil war had just ended. Richard's older brother, Edward, has become the ruler and we are now witnessing the celebration at the end of this dark period of these people's lives. Entering with this premise allows us to start mid-action, so that the famous opening to the play both makes sense and avoids seeming contrived. It's so hard to earn that right to break the silence as an actor anyway, but at the start of a play where nothing has preceded it – added to this the pressure that Martin Freeman [Richard III] is speaking one of Shakespeare's most famous lines – and there's a real danger of missing an opportunity to give us useful context straight away. Furthermore, it allows Martin to speak the first section as part of the scene so that the direct address becomes an element of surprise to the audience rather than something we take for granted. It's as if we're rewarded for buying into the context that we're presented with.

Day 17 (Week 4)

Today marked the next stage of rehearsals. We've tackled the play over two weeks, then over one week and now we're tackling each act over two days with the view to then go on next week and tackle it in one day and then run and note, run and note… It's a very effective and effortless way of getting familiar with the piece as a whole, I think. While it's often daunting to think of running a play, the idea of running it next week feels totally feasible because we've sort of been running it for the last four weeks, only over a longer period of time.

Today we implemented a few extra cuts in order to bring the playing time down (particularly for Part One). I jumped into a body bag to be the dead body in Act One, Scene Two. Apart from taking the opportunity to confirm that I never want to be in a body bag conscious again, it was also fascinating to have Lauren O'Neil [Lady Anne] and Martin Freeman spar over me on a gurney, especially with just my ears to guide me. Even with my eyes closed I could tell that the staging (still fluid at this stage) was the simplest it had been for this scene, but every move made sense, even when they chose not to hold their ground. At this stage, Jamie is beginning to build the transitions into the production. Some are simple, some are complex, but all of them are little opportunities to inject more storytelling, particularly during the early transitions. Jamie overlaps some of the scenes and therefore avoids transitions. In others, he establishes new characters. In one or two, they are very much used to clear a shitload of plates and teacups.

We've also had sound and music by the brilliant Ben and Max Ringham in the rehearsal room for about a week. Along with the rest of the production, Jamie and the Ringhams are constantly sculpting and defining the language for the sound and music in the show, giving everyone a real sense of progression as the tech looms just a week away and even less from our first runthrough of the play.

Finally I get to rub out the two or three (or ten!) variations of blocking I have in my script as we start to settle the staging for most scenes. That said, still nothing is being pinned down too tightly and the work is clearly better for it. Jamie gives the actors extraordinary freedom, whilst giving them clear boundaries. It means that each scene is alive and discovered as if for the first time, which is thrilling. The actors are still playing, but because of the early paraphrasing work, the sense of the story is now the core of their playing. Note to self: when directing a Shakespeare, paraphrase it. It's hugely worth it.

Day 26 (Week 5)

Today marks our last runthrough of the play before we begin tech. For the last few days there's been a different sort of focus in the room. The room flips from being ultra-concentrated one moment and then charged with a sense of pitched playfulness the next. We now run fight calls before each run. I've been involved with fight calls that take anywhere from thirty seconds to maybe five minutes. The fight call for this production of *Richard III* takes about twenty minutes!

There's no denying that every runthrough has been completely different. We've had glasses smash, knives flung into 'the audience', traffic jams and the odd word omitted. But there's also been a real 'other' feeling that has run through this entire final week of rehearsals (which has also seen us move to the beautiful Belsize Park area with yet more sunshine!) – and that powerful feeling has been the result of a combined effort of a company of people wanting to tell this story clearly and in a new, exciting way. It's a big risk, not least because we're defying many that claim Shakespeare's plays contain zero subtext. We are very much aiming to honour not just what Shakespeare wrote, but also everything Shakespeare didn't write; that which he left as fuel in the characters' veins, unexpressed, simmering beneath the surface, and implied within the fabric of his poetry.

For Jamie Lloyd Productions

Artistic Director	Jamie Lloyd
Executive Producer	Adam Speers
Assistant Producer	Emily Vaughan-Barrett
Head of Casting	Stuart Burt CDG
Marketing and General Management	Ambassador Theatre Group
Press	Emma Holland PR

This production of *Richard III* was first performed at the Trafalgar Studios, London, as part of the Trafalgar Transformed season, on 9 July 2014 (previews from 1 July), with the following cast, in alphabetical order:

ENSEMBLE	Alasdair Buchan
TYRREL	Simon Coombs
RICHMOND	Philip Cumbus
RICHARD	Martin Freeman
ENSEMBLE	Madeleine Harland
ENSEMBLE	Julie Jupp
CATESBY	Gerald Kyd
RIVERS	Joshua Lacey
LORD STANLEY	Paul Leonard
DUCHESS OF YORK	Gabrielle Lloyd
HASTINGS	Forbes Masson
KING EDWARD IV/ BISHOP OF ELY	Paul McEwan
QUEEN ELIZABETH	Gina McKee
CLARENCE/LORD MAYOR	Mark Meadows
DUKE OF NORFOLK/ ENSEMBLE	Vinta Morgan
LADY ANNE	Lauren O'Neil
QUEEN MARGARET	Maggie Steed
BUCKINGHAM	Jo Stone-Fewings

Director	Jamie Lloyd
Designer	Soutra Gilmour
Lighting Designer	Charles Balfour
Sound and Music	Ben and Max Ringham
Fight Director	Kate Waters
Voice and Text	Barbara Houseman
Video Designer	Duncan McLean
Wigs and Hair Designer	Richard Mawbey
Associate Director	Richard Fitch

RICHARD III

William Shakespeare

edited by Jamie Lloyd

Characters

RICHARD, DUKE OF GLOUCESTER, *later*
   KING RICHARD III
DUKE OF CLARENCE
CATESBY
LORD HASTINGS
LADY ANNE
QUEEN ELIZABETH
LORD RIVERS
DUKE OF BUCKINGHAM
LORD STANLEY
EARL OF RICHMOND
QUEEN MARGARET
TYRREL
KING EDWARD IV
DUCHESS OF YORK
DUKE OF YORK
PRINCE EDWARD
LORD MAYOR
BISHOP OF ELY
DUKE OF NORFOLK

This text went to press before the end of rehearsals and so may differ slightly from the play as performed.

ACT ONE

Scene One

RICHARD, DUKE OF GLOUCESTER.
    Now is the winter of our discontent
    Made glorious summer by this sun of York;
    And all the clouds that lour'd upon our house
    In the deep bosom of the ocean buried.
    Now are our brows bound with victorious wreaths,
    Our bruised arms hung up for monuments,
    Our stern alarums changed to merry meetings,
    Our dreadful marches to delightful measures.
    Grim-visaged War hath smooth'd his wrinkled front;
    And now, instead of mounting barbed steeds
    To fright the souls of fearful adversaries,
    He capers nimbly in a lady's chamber
    To the lascivious pleasing of a lute.
    But I, that am not shaped for sportive tricks,
    Nor made to court an amorous looking-glass;
    I, that am rudely stamp'd, and want love's majesty
    To strut before a wanton ambling nymph;
    I, that am curtail'd of this fair proportion,
    Cheated of feature by dissembling nature,
    Deformed, unfinish'd, sent before my time
    Into this breathing world, scarce half made up,
    And that so lamely and unfashionable
    That dogs bark at me as I halt by them –
    Why, I, in this weak piping time of peace,
    Have no delight to pass away the time,
    Unless to spy my shadow in the sun
    And descant on mine own deformity.
    And therefore, since I cannot prove a lover,
    To entertain these fair well-spoken days,
    I am determined to prove a villain

And hate the idle pleasures of these days.
Plots have I laid, inductions dangerous,
By drunken prophecies, libels and dreams,
To set my brother Clarence and the King
In deadly hate, the one against the other;
And if King Edward be as true and just
As I am subtle, false and treacherous,
This day should Clarence closely be mew'd up,
About a prophecy, which says that 'G'
Of Edward's heirs the murderer shall be.
Dive, thoughts, down to my soul: here Clarence comes.

Enter DUKE OF CLARENCE, *guarded*.

Brother, good day; what means this armed guard
That waits upon your grace?

CLARENCE.
                              His Majesty
Tendering my person's safety, hath appointed
This conduct to convey me to the Tower.

RICHARD.
Upon what cause?

CLARENCE.
                    Because my name is George.

RICHARD.
Alack, my lord, that fault is none of yours;
He should, for that, commit your godfathers.
But what's the matter, Clarence? May I know?

CLARENCE.
Yea, Richard, when I know; for I protest
As yet I do not: but, as I can learn,
He hearkens after prophecies and dreams;
And says a wizard told him that by 'G'
His issue disinherited should be.
And, for my name of George begins with 'G',
It follows in his thought that I am he.

RICHARD.
> Why, this it is, when men are ruled by women:
> 'Tis not the King that sends you to the Tower;
> Elizabeth, his wife, Clarence, 'tis she
> That tempers him to this extremity,
> That made him send Lord Hastings to the Tower,
> From whence this present day he is deliver'd.
> We are not safe, Clarence; we are not safe.

Enter CATESBY.

CATESBY.
> I beseech your graces both to pardon me;
> His Majesty hath straitly given in charge
> That no man shall have private conference,
> Of what degree soever, with his brother.

CLARENCE.
> We know thy charge, Catesby, and will obey.

RICHARD.
> We are the Queen's abjects, and must obey.
> Brother, farewell: I will unto the King;
> And whatsoever you will employ me in,
> Were it to call King Edward's woman 'sister',
> I will perform it to enfranchise you.
> Meantime, this deep disgrace in brotherhood
> Touches me deeper than you can imagine.

CLARENCE.
> I know it pleaseth neither of us well.

RICHARD.
> Well, your imprisonment shall not be long;
> Meantime, have patience.

CLARENCE.
> I must perforce. Farewell.

CLARENCE *and* GUARDS *exit*. CATESBY *lingers*.

RICHARD.
> Go, tread the path that thou shalt ne'er return.

Exit CATESBY.

Simple, plain Clarence! I do love thee so,
That I will shortly send thy soul to Heaven.
But who comes here? The new-deliver'd Hastings?

Enter LORD HASTINGS.

HASTINGS.
Good time of day unto my gracious lord!

RICHARD.
As much unto my good Lord Chamberlain!
Well are you welcome to the open air.
How hath your lordship brook'd imprisonment?

HASTINGS.
With patience, noble lord, as prisoners must:
But I shall live, my lord, to give them thanks
That were the cause of my imprisonment.

RICHARD.
No doubt, no doubt; and so shall Clarence too;
For they that were your enemies are his,
And have prevail'd as much on him as you.

HASTINGS.
More pity that the eagle should be mew'd,
While kites and buzzards prey at liberty.

RICHARD.
What news abroad?

HASTINGS.
No news so bad abroad as this at home:
The King is sickly, weak and melancholy,
And his physicians fear him mightily.

RICHARD.
Now, by St Paul, this news is bad indeed.
Where is he? In his bed?

HASTINGS.
He is.

RICHARD.
Go you before, and I will follow you.

Exit HASTINGS.

Edward cannot live, I hope; and must not die
Till George be pack'd with post-horse up to Heaven.
Which done, God take King Edward to his mercy,
And leave the world for me to bustle in!
For then I'll marry Warwick's youngest daughter.
What though I kill'd her husband and her father?
The readiest way to make the wench amends
Is to become her husband and her father.
But yet I run before my horse to market:
Clarence still breathes; Edward still lives and reigns.
When they are gone, then must I count my gains.

Exit.

Scene Two

Enter the corpse of Prince Edward of Lancaster; LADY ANNE
being the mourner.

ANNE.
Cursed be the hand that made these fatal holes.
Cursed be the heart that had the heart to do it.
Cursed the blood that let this blood from hence.
More direful hap betide that hated wretch
That makes us wretched by the death of thee,
Than I can wish to adders, spiders, toads,
Or any creeping venom'd thing that lives.
If ever he have wife, let her he made
As miserable by the death of him
As I am made by my poor husband's death.

Enter RICHARD.

Avaunt, thou dreadful minister of Hell!
Thou hadst but power over his mortal body,
His soul thou canst not have; therefore be gone.

RICHARD.
Sweet saint, for charity, be not so curst.

ANNE.
Foul devil, for God's sake, hence, and trouble us not;
For thou hast made the happy earth thy hell,
Fill'd it with cursing cries and deep exclaims.
If thou delight to view thy heinous deeds,
Behold this pattern of thy butcheries.

RICHARD.
O, gentle Anne –

ANNE.
                    O, see, see! his wounds
Open their congeal'd mouths and bleed afresh!
Blush, blush, thou lump of foul deformity,
For 'tis thy presence that exhales this blood
From cold and empty veins, where no blood dwells.
Thy deed, inhuman and unnatural,
Provokes this deluge most unnatural.
O God, which this blood madest, revenge his death!
Either Heaven with lightning strike the murderer dead,
Or earth, gape open wide and eat him quick.

RICHARD.
Lady, you know no rules of charity,
Which renders good for bad, blessings for curses.

ANNE.
Villain, thou know'st no law of God nor man.
No beast so fierce but knows some touch of pity.

RICHARD.
But I know none, and therefore am no beast.

ANNE.
O wonderful, when devils tell the truth!

RICHARD.
More wonderful, when angels are so angry.
Vouchsafe, divine perfection of a woman,
Of these supposed evils, to give me leave,
By circumstance, but to acquit myself.

ANNE.
Didst thou not kill my husband?

RICHARD.
I grant ye.

ANNE.
Dost grant me, hedgehog? Then, God grant me too
Thou mayst be damned for that wicked deed!
O, he was gentle, mild, and virtuous.

RICHARD.
The fitter for the King of Heaven, that hath him.

ANNE.
He is in Heaven, where thou shalt never come.

RICHARD.
Let him thank me, that holp to send him thither,
For he was fitter for that place than earth.

ANNE.
And thou unfit for any place but Hell.

RICHARD.
Yes, one place else, if you will hear me name it.

ANNE.
Some dungeon.

RICHARD.
Your bedchamber.
Your beauty was the cause of this effect;
Your beauty: which did haunt me in my sleep
To undertake the death of all the world,
So I might live one hour in your sweet bosom.

ANNE.
If I thought that, I tell thee, homicide,
These nails should rend that beauty from my cheeks.

RICHARD.
These eyes could not endure that beauty's wreck;
You should not blemish it, if I stood by:
As all the world is cheered by the sun,
So I by that. It is my day, my life.

ANNE.
Black night o'ershade thy day, and death thy life!

RICHARD.
He that bereft thee, lady, of thy husband,
Did it to help thee to a better husband!

ANNE.
His better doth not breathe upon the earth.

RICHARD.
He lives that loves thee better than he could.

ANNE.
Where is he?

RICHARD.
Here.

She spitteth at him.

Why dost thou spit at me?

ANNE.
Would it were mortal poison, for thy sake!

RICHARD.
Never came poison from so sweet a place.

ANNE.
Never hung poison on a fouler toad.
Out of my sight! thou dost infect my eyes.

RICHARD.
Thine eyes, sweet lady, have infected mine.

ANNE.

Would they were basilisks, to strike thee dead!

RICHARD.

I would they were, that I might die at once;
For now they kill me with a living death.
Those eyes of thine from mine have drawn salt tears,
Shamed their aspect with store of childish drops;
These eyes that never shed remorseful tear,
Thy beauty hath made them blind with weeping.
If thy revengeful heart cannot forgive,
Lo, here I lend thee this sharp-pointed blade;
Which if thou please to hide in this true bosom
And let the soul forth that adoreth thee.
I lay it naked to the deadly stroke,
And humbly beg the death upon my knee.

He lays his breast open: she offers at it with his sword.

Nay, do not pause; for I did kill King Henry,
But 'twas thy beauty that provoked me.
Nay, now dispatch; 'twas I that stabb'd young Edward,
But 'twas thy heavenly face that set me on.

Here she lets fall the blade.

Take up the blade again, or take up me.

ANNE.

Arise, dissembler: though I wish thy death,
I will not be thy executioner.

RICHARD.

Then bid me kill myself, and I will do it.

ANNE.

I have already.

RICHARD.

That was in thy rage:
Speak it again, and, even with the word,
That hand, which, for thy love, did kill thy love,
Shall, for thy love, kill a far truer love;
To both their deaths thou shalt be accessary.

ANNE.
  I would I knew thy heart.

RICHARD.
  'Tis figured in my tongue.

ANNE.
  I fear me both are false.

RICHARD.
  Then never man was true.

ANNE.
  Well, well, put down your blade.

RICHARD.
  Say, then, my peace is made.

ANNE.
  That shall you know hereafter.

RICHARD.
  But shall I live in hope?

ANNE.
  All men, I hope, live so.

RICHARD.
  Vouchsafe to wear this ring.

ANNE.
  To take is not to give.

RICHARD.
  Look how this ring encompasseth thy finger;
  Even so thy breast encloseth my poor heart.
  Wear both of them, for both of them are thine.
  And if thy poor devoted servant may
  But beg one favour at thy gracious hand,
  Thou dost confirm his happiness for ever.

ANNE.
  What is it?

RICHARD.

That it may please you to leave these sad designs
To him that hath most cause to be a mourner,
And after I have him solemnly interred
And wet his grave with my repentant tears,
I will with all expedient duty see you.

ANNE.

With all my heart; and much it joys me too,
To see you are become so penitent.

RICHARD.

Bid me farewell.

ANNE.

'Tis more than you deserve;
But since you teach me how to flatter you,
Imagine I have said farewell already.

Exit ANNE.

RICHARD.

Was ever woman in this humour woo'd?
Was ever woman in this humour won?
I'll have her; but I will not keep her long.
What? I, that kill'd her husband and his father,
To take her in her heart's extremest hate,
With curses in her mouth, tears in her eyes,
The bleeding witness of her hatred by;
Having God, her conscience, and these bars against me,
And I no friends to back my suit at all,
But the plain devil and dissembling looks?
And yet to win her, all the world to nothing!
Ha!
I do mistake my person all this while!
Upon my life, she finds, although I cannot,
Myself to be a marvellous proper man.
I'll be at charges for a looking-glass,
And entertain a score or two of tailors,
To study fashions to adorn my body:
Since I am crept in favour with myself,

I will maintain it with some little cost.
But first I'll turn yon fellow in his grave
And then return lamenting to my love.
Shine out, fair sun, till I have bought a glass,
That I may see my shadow as I pass.

Exit.

Scene Three

Enter QUEEN ELIZABETH *and* LORD RIVERS.

RIVERS.
Have patience, sister. There's no doubt His Majesty
Will soon recover his accustom'd health.

ELIZABETH.
If he were dead, what would betide of me?

RIVERS.
The heavens have bless'd you with a goodly son,
To be your comforter when he is gone.

ELIZABETH.
Oh, he is young and his minority
Is put unto the trust of Richard Gloucester,
A man that loves not me, nor you.

RIVERS.
Is it concluded that he shall be Protector?

ELIZABETH.
So it must be, if the King miscarry.

Enter the DUKE OF BUCKINGHAM *and* LORD
STANLEY, *with the* EARL OF RICHMOND.

BUCKINGHAM.
Good time of day unto your royal grace!

STANLEY.
God make Your Majesty joyful as you have been!

RIVERS.
Saw you the King today, my Lord Stanley?

STANLEY.
Richmond, the Duke of Buckingham and I
Are come from visiting His Majesty.

ELIZABETH.
What likelihood of his amendment, lords?

BUCKINGHAM.
Madam, good hope; his grace speaks cheerfully.

ELIZABETH.
God grant him health! Did you confer with him?

BUCKINGHAM.
Ay, madam; he desires to make atonement
Betwixt the Duke of Gloucester and your brother,
And sent to warn them to his royal presence.

ELIZABETH.
Would all were well! But that will never be;
I fear our happiness is at the highest.

Enter RICHARD *and* HASTINGS.

RICHARD.
Who are they that complain unto the King,
That I, forsooth, am stern, and love them not?
That fill his ears with such dissentious rumours?
Because I cannot flatter and speak fair,
Smile in men's faces, smooth, deceive and cog,
I must be held a rancorous enemy.
Cannot a plain man live and think no harm?

RIVERS.
To whom in all this presence speaks your grace?

RICHARD.
To thee, that hast nor honesty nor grace.
When have I injured thee? When done thee wrong?

Or thee? Or any of your faction?
A plague upon you all! His royal person,
Cannot be quiet scarce a breathing-while,
But you must trouble him with lewd complaints!

ELIZABETH.
Brother of Gloucester, you mistake the matter.
The King, of his own royal disposition,
And not provoked by any suitor else,
Makes him to send; that thereby he may gather
The ground of your ill will, and so remove it.

RICHARD.
I cannot tell: the world is grown so bad,
That wrens make prey where eagles dare not perch.

ELIZABETH.
Come, come, we know your meaning, brother Gloucester;
You envy my advancement and my friends':
God grant we never may have need of you!

RICHARD.
Meantime, God grants that we have need of you:
My brother is imprison'd by your means,
Myself disgraced, and the nobility
Held in contempt; whilst many fair promotions
Are daily given to ennoble those
That scarce, some two days since, were worth a noble.

ELIZABETH.
I never did incense His Majesty
Against the Duke of Clarence, but have been
An earnest advocate to plead for him.
My lord, you do me shameful injury,
Falsely to draw me in these vile suspects.

RICHARD.
You may deny that you were not the cause
Of my Lord Hastings' late imprisonment.

RIVERS.
She may, my lord, for –

RICHARD.

    She may, Lord Rivers! why, who knows not so?
    She may do more, sir, than denying that:
    She may help you to many fair preferments,
    And then deny her aiding hand therein
    And lay those honours on your high desert.
    What may she not? She may, yea, marry, may she –

RIVERS.

    What, marry, may she?

RICHARD.

    What, marry, may she? Marry with a king!

ELIZABETH.

    My Lord of Gloucester, I have too long borne
    Your blunt upbraidings and your bitter scoffs.
    I had rather be a country servant-maid
    Than a great queen, with this condition,
    To be thus taunted, scorn'd, and baited at.
    By Heaven, I will acquaint His Majesty
    With those gross taunts that oft I have endured.

RICHARD.

    Tell him. And spare not. Look, what I have said
    I will avouch in presence of the King:
    I dare adventure to be sent to the Tower.
    'Tis time to speak; my pains are quite forgot.
    Ere you were queen, yea, or your husband king,
    I was a packhorse in his great affairs,
    A weeder-out of his proud adversaries,
    A liberal rewarder of his friends:
    To royalise his blood I spilt mine own.
    In all which time you and your brother here
    Were factious for the house of Lancaster.
    Let me put in your minds, if you forget,
    What you have been ere now, and what you are;
    Withal, what I have been, and what I am.

RIVERS.

    My Lord of Gloucester, in those busy days
    Which here you urge to prove us enemies,

We follow'd then our lord, our lawful king.
So should we you, if you should be our king.

RICHARD.
If I should be! I had rather be a pedlar:
Far be it from my heart, the thought of it!
I am too childish-foolish for this world.

Enter QUEEN MARGARET.

MARGARET.
Hear me, you wrangling pirates, that fall out
In sharing that which you have pill'd from me!
Which of you trembles not that looks on me?
If not, that, I being Queen, you bow like subjects,
Yet that, by you deposed, you quake like rebels.
O gentle villain, do not turn away!

RICHARD.
Foul wrinkled witch, what makest thou in my sight?
Wert thou not banished on pain of death?

MARGARET.
I was; but I do find more pain in banishment
Than death can yield me here by my abode.
A husband and a son thou owest to me;
And thou a kingdom; all of you allegiance.
The sorrow that I have, by right is yours,
And all the pleasures you usurp are mine.
Give way, dull clouds, to my quick curses!
If not by war, by surfeit die your king,
As ours by murder, to make him a king!
Edward thy son, which now is Prince of Wales,
For Edward my son, which was Prince of Wales,
Die in his youth by like untimely violence!
Thyself a queen, for me that was a queen,
Outlive thy glory, like my wretched self!
Long mayst thou live to wail thy children's death,
And see another, as I see thee now,
Deck'd in thy rights, as thou art stall'd in mine!
Long die thy happy days before thy death,

And, after many lengthen'd hours of grief,
Die neither mother, wife, nor England's queen!
Rivers and Hastings, you were standers-by
When my son
Was stabb'd with bloody daggers: God, I pray him,
That none of you may live your natural age,
But by some unlook'd accident cut off!

RICHARD.
Have done thy charm, thou hateful wither'd hag!

MARGARET.
And leave out thee? Stay, dog, for thou shalt hear me.
If Heaven have any grievous plague in store
Exceeding those that I can wish upon thee,
O, let them keep it till thy sins be ripe,
And then hurl down their indignation
On thee, the troubler of the poor world's peace.
The worm of conscience still begnaw thy soul;
Thy friends suspect for traitors while thou liv'st,
And take deep traitors for thy dearest friends.
No sleep close up that deadly eye of thine,
Unless it be whilst some tormenting dream
Affrights thee with a hell of ugly devils.
Thou elvish-mark'd, abortive, rooting hog,
Thou that wast seal'd in thy nativity
The slave of nature and the son of Hell;
Thou slander of thy mother's heavy womb,
Thou loathed issue of thy father's loins,
Thou rag of honour, thou detested –

RICHARD.
Margaret.

MARGARET.
          Richard!

RICHARD.
                    Yes?

MARGARET.
                    I call'd thee not.

RICHARD.
    I cry thee mercy then, for I did think
    That thou hadst called me all these bitter names.

MARGARET.
    Why, so I did, but looked for no reply.
    O, let me make the period to my curse.

GLOUCESTER.
    'Tis done by me and ends in 'Margaret'.

ELIZABETH.
    Thus have you breathed your curse against yourself.

MARGARET.
    Poor painted queen, vain flourish of my fortune,
    The day will come that thou shalt wish for me
    To help thee curse this poisonous bunch-backed toad.

HASTINGS.
    False-boding woman, end thy woeful curse,
    Lest to thy harm thou move our patience.

RIVERS.
    Dispute not with her; she is lunatic.

MARGARET.
    O, that your young nobility could judge
    What 'twere to lose it and be miserable.

BUCKINGHAM.
    Have done, have done.

MARGARET.
    O Buckingham, take heed of yonder dog!
    Look, when he fawns, he bites; and when he bites,
    His venom tooth will rankle to the death.
    Have not to do with him! Beware of him!

RICHARD.
    What doth she say, my Lord of Buckingham?

BUCKINGHAM.
    Nothing that I respect, my gracious lord.

MARGARET.
>What, dost thou scorn me for my gentle counsel?
>And soothe the devil that I warn thee from?
>O, but remember this another day,
>When he shall split thy very heart with sorrow,
>And say poor Margaret was a prophetess!
>Live each of you the subjects to his hate,
>And he to yours, and all of you to God's.

>*Exit.*

HASTINGS.
>My hair doth stand on end to hear her curses.

RIVERS.
>And so doth mine. I muse why she's at liberty.

RICHARD.
>I cannot blame her; by God's holy mother,
>She hath had too much wrong, and I repent
>My part thereof that I have done to her.

ELIZABETH.
>I never did her any, to my knowledge.

RICHARD.
>But you have all the vantage of her wrong.

BUCKINGHAM.
>Madam, His Majesty doth call for you.

ELIZABETH.
>Buckingham, we come. Lords, will you go with us?

RIVERS.
>Madam, we will attend your grace.

>*Exeunt all but* RICHARD.

RICHARD.
>I do the wrong, and first begin to brawl.
>The secret mischiefs that I set abroach,
>I lay unto the grievous charge of others.

>*Enter* TYRREL.

But, soft, here comes my executioner.
How now, my hardy, stout resolved mates!
Are you now going to dispatch this deed?

TYRREL.
I am, my lord; and come to have the warrant
That I may be admitted where he is.

RICHARD.
Well thought upon; I have it here about me.

Gives the warrant.

But, sir, be sudden in the execution,
Withal obdurate, do not hear him plead;
For Clarence is well-spoken, and perhaps
May move your hearts to pity if you mark him.

TYRREL.
Fear not, my lord, I will not stand to prate.
Talkers are no good doers; be assured
I come to use my hands and not my tongue.

RICHARD.
Your eyes drop millstones, when fools' eyes drop tears:
I like you, lad. About your business straight;
Go, go, dispatch.

TYRREL.
                    I will, my noble lord.

Exeunt.

Scene Four

Enter CLARENCE *with* CATESBY.

CATESBY.
    Why looks your grace so heavily today?

CLARENCE.
    O, I have pass'd a miserable night,
    So full of ugly sights, of ghastly dreams.
    I would not spend another such a night,
    Though 'twere to buy a world of happy days,
    So full of dismal terror was the time!

CATESBY.
    What was your dream? I long to hear you tell it.

CLARENCE.
    Methoughts that I had broken from the Tower,
    And was embark'd to cross to Burgundy;
    And, in my company, my brother Gloucester;
    Who from my cabin tempted me to walk
    Upon the hatches: thence we looked toward England,
    And cited up a thousand fearful times,
    During the wars of York and Lancaster
    That had befall'n us. As we paced along
    Upon the giddy footing of the hatches,
    Methought that Gloucester stumbled; and, in falling,
    (The thought to steady him) struck me overboard,
    Into the tumbling billows of the main.
    O, Lord! Methought what pain it was to drown,
    What dreadful noise of waters in mine ears,
    What ugly sights of death within mine eyes.
    Methought I saw a thousand fearful wrecks;
    Ten thousand men that fishes gnaw'd upon;
    Wedges of gold, great anchors, heaps of pearl,
    Inestimable stones, unvalued jewels,
    All scatter'd in the bottom of the sea.
    Some lay in dead men's skulls, and, in those holes
    Where eyes did once inhabit, there were crept,
    As 'twere in scorn of eyes, reflecting gems,

That woo'd the slimy bottom of the deep,
And mock'd the dead bones that lay scatter'd by.

CATESBY.
Had you such leisure in the time of death
To gaze upon the secrets of the deep?

CLARENCE.
Methought I had; and often did I strive
To yield the ghost, but still the envious flood
Stopp'd in my soul, and would not let it forth
To seek the empty, vast and wandering air;
But smother'd it within my panting bulk,
Which almost burst to belch it in the sea.

CATESBY.
Awaked you not with this sore agony?

CLARENCE.
O, no, my dream was lengthen'd after life.
O, then began the tempest to my soul.
I pass'd, methought, the melancholy flood,
With that grim ferryman which poets write of,
Unto the kingdom of perpetual night.
Then there did greet my stranger soul,
A shadow like an angel, with bright hair
Dabbled in blood; and he shrieked out aloud:
'Clarence is come; false, fleeting, perjured Clarence,
That stabb'd me in the field by Tewksbury;
Seize on him, Furies, take him unto torment!'
With that, methoughts, a legion of foul fiends
Environ'd me about, and howled in mine ears
Such hideous cries, that with the very noise
I, trembling, waked, and for a season after
Could not believe but that I was in Hell,
Such terrible impression made my dream.

CATESBY.
No marvel, my lord, that it affrighted you;
I promise, I am afraid to hear you tell it.

CLARENCE.
 O Catesby, I have done those things,
 Which now bear evidence against my soul,
 For Edward's sake; and see how he requites me!
 My soul is heavy, and I fain would sleep.

CATESBY.
 And so, my lord: God give your grace good rest!

CLARENCE *sleeps*.

 Sorrow breaks seasons and reposing hours,
 Makes the night morning, and the noontide night.

Enter TYRREL.

TYRREL.
 What, shall we stab him as he sleeps?

CATESBY.
 No; then he will say 'twas done cowardly, when he wakes.

TYRREL.
 When he wakes? Why, fool, he shall never wake till
 Judgement Day.

CATESBY.
 Why, then he will say we stabbed him sleeping.

TYRREL.
 The urging of that word 'Judgement' hath bred a kind of
 remorse in me.

CATESBY.
 What, art thou afraid?

TYRREL.
 Not to kill him, having a warrant for it; but to be damned for
 killing him, from which no warrant can defend us.

CATESBY.
 I thought thou hadst been resolute.

TYRREL.
 So I am, to let him live.

CATESBY.
Back to the Duke of Gloucester and tell him so.

TYRREL.
I pray thee, stay a while: I hope my holy humour will
change.

CATESBY.
How dost thou feel thyself now?

TYRREL.
'Faith, some certain dregs of conscience are yet within me.

CATESBY.
Remember our reward when the deed is done.

TYRREL.
Zounds, he dies: I had forgot the reward.

CATESBY.
Where is thy conscience now?

TYRREL.
In the Duke of Gloucester's purse.

CATESBY.
So when he opens his purse to give us our reward, thy
conscience flies out.

TYRREL.
Let it go; there's few or none will entertain it.

CATESBY.
How if it come to thee again?

TYRREL.
I'll not meddle with it: it is a dangerous thing: it makes a
man a coward: a man cannot steal, but it accuseth him; he
cannot swear, but it checks him; he cannot lie with his
neighbour's wife, but it detects him: 'tis a blushing
shamefaced spirit that mutinies in a man's bosom; it fills one
full of obstacles.

CLARENCE *awakes*. CATESBY *hides*.

CLARENCE.
In God's name, what art thou?

TYRREL.
A man, as you are.

CLARENCE.
But not, as I am, royal.

TYRREL.
Nor you, as I am, loyal.

CLARENCE.
Who sent you hither? Wherefore do you come?

TYRREL.
To, to –

CLARENCE.
To murder me?

Re-enter CATESBY.

CATESBY.
Ay.

CLARENCE.
You scarcely have the hearts to tell me so,
And therefore cannot have the hearts to do it.
Wherein, my friend, have I offended you?

CATESBY.
Offended us you have not, but the King.

CLARENCE.
I shall be reconciled to him again.

TYRREL.
Never, my lord; therefore prepare to die.

CLARENCE.
Are you drawn forth among a world of men
To slay the innocent? What is my offence?
Where is the evidence that doth accuse me?
Before I be convict by course of law,
To threaten me with death is most unlawful.

CATESBY.
What we will do, we do upon command.

TYRREL.
And he that hath commanded is the King.

CLARENCE.
Erroneous vassal! The great king of kings
Hath in the tables of His law commanded
That thou shalt do no murder: and wilt thou, then,
Spurn at his edict and fulfil a man's?
Take heed; for He holds vengeance in His hands,
To hurl upon their heads that break his law.

CATESBY.
And that same vengeance doth He hurl on thee
For false forswearing and for murder too.

CLARENCE.
Alas! For whose sake did I that ill deed?
For Edward, for my brother, for his sake.
He sends you not to murder me for this,
For in that sin he is as deep as I.
If you be hired for meed, go back again,
And I will send you to my brother Gloucester,
Who shall reward you better for my life
Than Edward will for tidings of my death.

CATESBY.
You are deceived, your brother Gloucester hates you.

CLARENCE.
O, do not slander him, for he is kind.

CATESBY.
Right,
As snow in harvest. Thou deceivest thyself:
'Tis he that sent us hither now to slaughter thee.

CLARENCE.
It cannot be; for when I parted with him,
He hugg'd me in his arms, and swore, with sobs,
That he would labour my delivery.

CATESBY.
> Why, so he doth, now he delivers thee
> From this world's thraldom to the joys of Heaven.

TYRREL.
> Make peace with God, for you must die, my lord.

CLARENCE.
> Hast thou that holy feeling in thy soul,
> To counsel me to make my peace with God,
> And art thou yet to thy own soul so blind,
> That thou wilt war with God by murdering me?

TYRREL.
> What shall we do?

CLARENCE.
> Relent, and save your souls.

CATESBY.
> Relent! 'Tis cowardly and womanish.

CLARENCE.
> Not to relent is beastly, savage, devilish.
> My friend, I spy some pity in thy looks:
> O, if thine eye be not a flatterer,
> Come thou on my side, and entreat for me!

> CLARENCE *is murdered*.

TYRREL.
> A bloody deed, and desperately dispatched.
> How fain, like Pilate, would I wash my hands
> Of this most grievous guilty murder done!

> *Exeunt*.

ACT TWO

Scene One

Enter KING EDWARD IV, *sick,* ELIZABETH, RIVERS,
HASTINGS, BUCKINGHAM *and others*.

KING EDWARD IV.
Why, so. Now have I done a good day's work.
You peers, continue this united league.
And more in peace my soul shall part to Heaven,
Since I have set my friends at peace on earth
Hastings and Rivers, take each other's hand.
Dissemble not your hatred, swear you love.

RIVERS.
By Heaven, my heart is purged from grudging hate,
And with my hand I seal my true heart's love.

HASTINGS.
So thrive I, as I truly swear the like!

KING EDWARD IV.
Madam, yourself are not exempt in this.
Wife, love Lord Hastings, let him kiss your hand;
And what you do, do it unfeignedly.

ELIZABETH.
Here, Hastings; I will never more remember
Our former hatred, so thrive I and mine!

They embrace.

KING EDWARD IV.
Now, princely Buckingham, seal thou this league
With thy embracements to my wife's ally,
And make me happy in your unity.

BUCKINGHAM.
>   Whenever Buckingham doth turn his hate
>   Upon your grace, but with duteous love
>   Doth cherish you and yours, God punish me
>   With hate in those where I expect most love.
>   When I have most need to employ a friend,
>   And most assured that he is a friend,
>   Deep, hollow, treacherous, and full of guile
>   Be he unto me! This do I beg of God,
>   When I am cold in zeal to yours.

KING EDWARD IV.
>   A pleasing cordial, princely Buckingham,
>   Is this thy vow unto my sickly heart.
>   There wanteth now our brother Gloucester here,
>   To make the perfect period of this peace.

>   *Enter* RICHARD.

RICHARD.
>   Good morrow to my sovereign King and Queen!

BUCKINGHAM.
>   And, in good time, here comes the noble duke.

RICHARD.
>   And, princely peers, a happy time of day!

KING EDWARD IV.
>   Brother, we have done deeds of charity;
>   Made peace of enmity, fair love of hate,
>   Between these swelling, wrong-incensed peers.

RICHARD.
>   A blessed labour, my most sovereign liege.
>   Amongst this princely heap, if any here,
>   By false intelligence, or wrong surmise,
>   Hold me a foe;
>   If I unwittingly, or in my rage,
>   Have aught committed that is hardly borne,
>   By any in this presence, I desire
>   To reconcile me to his friendly peace:

'Tis death to me to be at enmity;
I hate it, and desire all good men's love.
First, madam, I entreat true peace of you,
Which I will purchase with my duteous service;
Of you, Lord Rivers,
That without desert have frown'd on me;
Lords, gentlemen; indeed, of all.
I do not know that Englishman alive
With whom my soul is any jot at odds
More than the infant that is born tonight.
I thank my God for my humility.

ELIZABETH.
I would to God all strifes were well compounded.
My sovereign liege, I do beseech Your Majesty
To take our brother Clarence to your grace.

RICHARD.
Why, madam, have I offer'd love for this,
To be so flouted in this royal presence?
Who knows not that the gentle Duke is dead?

They all start.

You do him injury to scorn his corpse.

RIVERS.
Who knows not he is dead? Who knows he is?

ELIZABETH.
All-seeing Heaven, what a world is this?

KING EDWARD IV.
Is Clarence dead? The order was reversed.

RICHARD.
But he, poor soul, by your first order died,
And that a winged Mercury did bear:
Some tardy cripple bore the countermand.
That came too lag to see him buried.

KING EDWARD IV.
Have I a tongue to doom my brother's death?
His crime was thought

And yet his punishment was bitter death.
Who sued to me for him? Who, in my rage,
Kneel'd at my feet, and bade me be advised?
Who spake of brotherhood? Who spake of love?
Who told me, when we both lay in the field
Frozen almost to death, how he did lap me
Even in his own garments, and gave himself,
All thin and naked, to the numb cold night?
All this from my remembrance brutish wrath
Sinfully pluck'd, and not a man of you
Had so much grace to put it in my mind.
The proudest of you all
Have been beholding to him in his life;
Yet none of you would once plead for his life.
O God, I fear Thy justice will take hold
On me, and you, and mine, and yours for this!
Come, Hastings, help me to my closet.
Oh, poor Clarence!

Exeunt some with KING EDWARD IV *and* ELIZABETH.

RICHARD.
This is the fruit of rashness! Mark'd you not
How that the guilty brother of the Queen
Look'd pale when he did hear of Clarence' death?
O, he did urge it still unto the King!
God will revenge it. But come, let us in,
To comfort Edward with our company.

BUCKINGHAM.
I wait upon your grace.

Exeunt.

Scene Two

Enter the DUCHESS *of* YORK. *Enter* ELIZABETH, *with her hair about her ears.*

ELIZABETH.
Oh, who shall hinder me to wail and weep,
To chide my fortune, and torment myself?
I'll join with black despair against my soul,
And to myself become an enemy.

DUCHESS OF YORK.
What means this scene of rude impatience?

ELIZABETH.
To make an act of tragic violence:
Edward, my lord, your son, our King, is dead.

DUCHESS OF YORK.
Alas, I am the mother of these moans!
Pour all your tears! I am your sorrow's nurse.
Thou art a widow; yet thou art a mother,
And hast the comfort of thy children left thee.
But death hath snatch'd my husband from mine arms,
And pluck'd two crutches from my feeble limbs,
Edward and Clarence.

Enter RICHARD, RIVERS, BUCKINGHAM, STANLEY, HASTINGS *and* RICHMOND.

RICHARD.
Sister, have comfort: all of us have cause
To wail the dimming of our shining star.

BUCKINGHAM.
Though we have spent our harvest of this king,
We are to reap the harvest of his son.

RIVERS.
Madam, bethink you, like a careful mother,
Of the young prince your son: send straight for him;
Let him be crown'd. In him your comfort lives:
Drown desperate sorrow in dead Edward's grave,
And plant your joys in living Edward's throne.

BUCKINGHAM.
>Me seemeth good, that, with some little train,
>Forthwith from Ludlow the young prince be fetch'd
>Hither to London, to be crown'd our king.

RIVERS.
>Why with some little train, my Lord of Buckingham?

BUCKINGHAM.
>Marry, my lord, lest, by a multitude,
>The new-heal'd wound of malice should break out.
>Which would be so much the more dangerous
>By how much the state is green and yet ungovern'd.

RICHARD.
>I hope the King made peace with all of us
>And the compact is firm and true in me.

RIVERS.
>And so in me; and so, I think, in all:
>Therefore I say with noble Buckingham,
>That it is meet so few should fetch the Prince.

HASTINGS.
>And so say I.

RICHARD.
>Then be it so –

RIVERS.
>   And go we to determine
>Who they shall be that straight shall post to Ludlow.

Exeunt all except DUCHESS OF YORK, RICHARD *and*
BUCKINGHAM.

DUCHESS OF YORK.
>I have bewept a worthy husband's death,
>And lived by looking on his images:
>But now two mirrors of his princely semblance
>Are crack'd in pieces by malignant death,
>And I for comfort have but one false glass,
>Which grieves me when I see my shame in him.

RICHARD.
  Madam, my mother, I do humbly crave your blessing.

DUCHESS OF YORK.
  God bless thee; and put meekness in thy mind,
  Love, charity, obedience, and true duty!

  Exit DUCHESS OF YORK.

RICHARD.
  Amen; and make me die a good old man!
  That is the butt-end of a mother's blessing:
  I marvel why her grace did leave it out.
  For God's sake, let not us two stay at home.

BUCKINGHAM.
  Lord Protector, I'll sort occasion,
  As index to the story we late talk'd of,
  To part the Queen's proud brother from the Prince.

RICHARD.
  My other self, my counsel's consistory,
  My oracle, my prophet! My dear cousin,
  I, like a child, will go by thy direction.
  Towards Ludlow then, for we'll not stay behind.

  Exeunt.

Scene Three

Enter young YORK, ELIZABETH, *and the* DUCHESS OF
YORK.

DUCHESS OF YORK.
  I long with all my heart to see the Prince:
  I hope he is much grown since last I saw him.

ELIZABETH.
  But I hear, no; they say my son of York
  Hath almost overta'en him in his growth.

YORK.

Ay, Mother; but I would not have it so.

DUCHESS OF YORK.

Why, my young grandson, it is good to grow.

YORK.

Grandam, one night, as we did sit at supper,
My uncle Rivers talk'd how I did grow
More than my brother: 'Ay,' quoth my uncle Gloucester,
'Small herbs have grace, great weeds do grow apace':
And since, methinks, I would not grow so fast,
Because sweet flowers are slow and weeds make haste.

DUCHESS OF YORK.

Good faith, good faith, the saying did not hold
In him that did object the same to thee;
He was the wretched'st thing when he was young,
So long a-growing and so leisurely,
That, if this rule were true, he should be gracious.

YORK.

Marry, they say my uncle grew so fast
That he could gnaw a crust at two hours old.

ELIZABETH.

A parlous boy: go to, you are too shrewd.

DUCHESS OF YORK.

Good madam, be not angry with the child.

ELIZABETH.

Pitchers have ears.

Enter STANLEY *and* RICHMOND.

What news?

STANLEY.

Such news, madam, as grieves me to unfold.

ELIZABETH.

How fares the Prince?

RICHMOND.

      Well, madam, and in health.

DUCHESS OF YORK.
What is thy news then?

STANLEY.
Lord Rivers is sent to Pomfret, a prisoner.

DUCHESS OF YORK.
Who hath committed him?

RICHMOND.
                              The mighty Dukes,
Gloucester and Buckingham.

ELIZABETH.
                              For what offence?

STANLEY.
The sum of all we can, we have disclosed.

ELIZABETH.
Ay me, I see the downfall of our house!
The tiger now hath seized the gentle hind;
Welcome destruction, blood and massacre.
I see, as in a map, the end of all.

Exeunt.

ACT THREE

Scene One

Enter the young PRINCE EDWARD, RICHARD *and*
BUCKINGHAM.

BUCKINGHAM.
Welcome, sweet Prince, to London.

RICHARD.
Welcome, dear cousin, my thoughts' sovereign.
The weary way hath made you melancholy.

PRINCE EDWARD.
No, uncle, but our crosses on the way
Have made it tedious, wearisome, and heavy.
I want more uncles here to welcome me.

RICHARD.
Sweet Prince, the untainted virtue of your years
Hath not yet dived into the world's deceit.
That uncle which you want was dangerous;
Your grace attended to his sugar'd words,
But look'd not on the poison of his heart:
God keep you from him, and from such false friends!

PRINCE EDWARD.
God keep me from false friends, but he was none.

Enter CATESBY, *with the* LORD MAYOR.

CATESBY.
My lord, the Mayor of London comes to greet you.

LORD MAYOR.
God bless your grace with health and happy days!

PRINCE EDWARD.
I thank you, good my lord.
I thought my mother, and my brother York,

Would long ere this have met us on the way
Fie, what a slug is Hastings, that he comes not
To tell us whether they will come or no!

Enter HASTINGS *with* BISHOP OF ELY.

BUCKINGHAM.
And, in good time, here comes the sweating lord.

PRINCE EDWARD.
Welcome, my lord: what, will our mother come?

HASTINGS.
On what occasion, God he knows, not I,
The Queen your mother, and your brother York,
Have taken sanctuary. The tender Prince
Would fain have come with me to meet your grace,
But by his mother was perforce withheld.

BUCKINGHAM.
Fie, what an indirect and peevish course
Is this of hers! Lord Ely, will your grace
Persuade the Queen to send the Duke of York
Unto his princely brother presently?
If she deny, Lord Hastings, go with him,
And from her jealous arms pluck him perforce.

BISHOP OF ELY.
My Lord of Buckingham, if my weak oratory
Can from his mother win the Duke of York,
Anon expect him here; but if she be obdurate
To mild entreaties, God in heaven forbid
We should infringe the holy privilege
Of blessed sanctuary!

BUCKINGHAM.
You are too senseless-obstinate, my lord;
Too ceremonious and traditional.
You break no privilege nor charter there.
Oft have I heard of sanctuary men;
But sanctuary children ne'er till now.

PRINCE EDWARD.
Good lord, make all the speedy haste you may.

BISHOP OF ELY.
My lord, you shall o'er-rule my mind for once.
Come on, Lord Hastings, will you go with me?

Exit ELY *and* HASTINGS.

PRINCE EDWARD.
Where shall we sojourn till our coronation?

RICHARD.
Where it seems best unto your royal self.
If I may counsel you, some day or two
Your Highness shall repose you at the Tower;
Then where you please, and shall be thought most fit
For your best health and recreation.

PRINCE EDWARD.
I do not like the Tower, of any place.

BUCKINGHAM.
Now, in good time, here comes the Duke of York.

Enter young YORK, HASTINGS *and* BISHOP OF ELY.

PRINCE EDWARD.
Richard of York! How fares our loving brother?

YORK.
Well, my dread lord; so must I call you now.

PRINCE EDWARD.
Ay, brother, to our grief, as it is yours.

RICHARD.
How fares our cousin, noble Lord of York?

YORK.
I thank you, gentle uncle. O, my lord,
You said that idle weeds are fast in growth.
The Prince my brother hath outgrown me far.

RICHARD.
　He hath, my lord.

YORK.
　　　　　　　　And therefore is he idle?

RICHARD.
　O, my fair cousin, I must not say so.

YORK.
　Then is he more beholding to you than I.

RICHARD.
　He may command me as my sovereign,
　But you have power in me as in a kinsman.

YORK.
　I pray you, Uncle, give me your dagger.

RICHARD.
　What, would you have my weapon, little lord?

YORK.
　I would, that I might thank you as you call me.

RICHARD.
　How?

YORK.
　Little.

PRINCE EDWARD.
　My Lord of York will still be cross in talk:
　Uncle, your grace knows how to bear with him.

YORK.
　You mean, to bear me, not to bear with me.
　Uncle, my brother mocks both you and me;
　Because that I am little, like an ape,
　He thinks that you should bear me on your shoulders.

BUCKINGHAM.
　With what a sharp-provided wit he reasons:
　To mitigate the scorn he gives his uncle,
　He prettily and aptly taunts himself:
　So cunning and so young is wonderful.

RICHARD (*aside*).
>So wise so young, they say, do never live long.
>My lord, will't please you pass along?
>Myself and my good cousin Buckingham
>Will to your mother, to entreat of her
>To meet you at the Tower and welcome you.

YORK.
>What, will you go unto the Tower, my lord?

PRINCE EDWARD.
>My Lord Protector needs will have it so.

YORK.
>I shall not sleep in quiet at the Tower.

RICHARD.
>Why, what should you fear?

YORK.
>Marry, my uncle Clarence' angry ghost:
>My grandam told me he was murdered there.

PRINCE EDWARD.
>I fear no uncles dead.

RICHARD.
>Nor none that live, I hope.

>*Exeunt all but* RICHARD, BUCKINGHAM *and* CATESBY.

BUCKINGHAM.
>Think you, my lord, this little prating York
>Was not incensed by his subtle mother
>To taunt and scorn you thus opprobriously?

RICHARD.
>No doubt, no doubt; O, 'tis a perilous boy.
>He is all the mother's, from the top to toe.

BUCKINGHAM.
>Well, let them rest. Come hither, Catesby.
>What think'st thou? Is it not an easy matter
>To make William, Lord Hastings, of our mind,

> For the instalment of this noble Duke
> In the seat royal of this famous isle?

CATESBY.
> He for King Edward's sake so loves the Prince,
> That he will not be won to aught against him.

BUCKINGHAM.
> What think'st thou, then, of Stanley? What will he?

CATESBY.
> He will do all in all as Hastings doth.

BUCKINGHAM.
> Well, then, no more but this: go, gentle Catesby,
> And, as it were far off sound thou Lord Hastings
> How doth he stand affected to our purpose
> And summon him
> To sit about the coronation.
> If thou dost find him tractable to us,
> Encourage him, and tell him all our reasons:
> If he be leaden, icy-cold, unwilling,
> Be thou so too; and so break off your talk,
> And give us notice of his inclination.

RICHARD.
> Shall we hear from you, Catesby, ere we sleep?

CATESBY.
> You shall, my lord.

> *Exit* CATESBY.

BUCKINGHAM.
> Now, my lord, what shall we do, if we perceive
> Lord Hastings will not yield to our complots?

RICHARD.
> Chop off his head; something we will determine.
> And, look, when I am King, claim thou of me
> The earldom of Hereford, and the moveables
> Whereof the King my brother was possess'd.

BUCKINGHAM.
I'll claim that promise at your grace's hands.

RICHARD.
And look to have it yielded with all kindness.

Exeunt.

Scene Two

Enter HASTINGS. *Enter* RICHMOND.

HASTINGS.
Richmond? What is't o'clock?

RICHMOND.
Upon the stroke of four. I bring a message from Lord Stanley.

HASTINGS.
Cannot he sleep these tedious nights?

RICHMOND.
So it should seem by that I have to say.
He dreamt tonight the boar had razed his helm.
Therefore he sends to know your lordship's pleasure,
If presently you will take horse with him,
And with all speed post with him toward the north,
To shun the danger that his soul divines.

HASTINGS.
Go, Richmond, go, return unto Lord Stanley;
I wonder he is so fond to trust
The mockery of unquiet slumbers.
To fly the boar before the boar pursues
Were to incense the boar to follow us
And make pursuit where he did mean no chase.
Go, bid Lord Stanley rise and come to me
And we will both together to the Tower,
Where he shall see the boar will use us kindly.

RICHMOND.
My gracious lord, I'll tell him what you say.

Exit RICHMOND.

Enter CATESBY.

CATESBY.
Many good morrows to my noble lord!

HASTINGS.
Good morrow, Catesby; you are early stirring.
What news, what news, in this our tottering state?

CATESBY.
It is a reeling world indeed, my lord;
And I believe 'twill never stand upright
Till Richard wear the garland of the realm.

HASTINGS.
How? Wear the garland? Dost thou mean the crown?

CATESBY.
Ay, my good lord.

HASTINGS.
I'll have this crown of mine cut from my shoulders
Ere I will see the crown so foul misplaced.
But canst thou guess that he doth aim at it?

CATESBY.
Ay, on my life; and hopes to find you forward
Upon his party for the gain thereof;
And thereupon he sends you this good news,
That this same very day your enemy,
The brother of the Queen, must die at Pomfret.

HASTINGS.
Indeed, I am no mourner for that news,
Because he has been still mine enemy.
But, that I'll give my voice on Richard's side,
To bar my master's heirs in true descent,
God knows I will not do it, to the death.

CATESBY.
God keep your lordship in that gracious mind!

HASTINGS.
I tell thee, Catesby –

CATESBY.
What, my lord?

HASTINGS.
Ere a fortnight make me older,
I'll send some packing that yet think not on it.

CATESBY.
'Tis a vile thing to die, my gracious lord,
When men are unprepared and look not for it.

HASTINGS.
O monstrous, monstrous! And so falls it out
With some men else, who think themselves as safe
As thou and I – who, as thou know'st, are dear
To princely Richard and to Buckingham.

CATESBY.
The Princes both make high account of you.

HASTINGS.
I know they do, and I have well deserved it.

Exit CATESBY.

Enter STANLEY *and* RICHMOND.

Come on, come on; where is your boar-spear, man?
Fear you the boar, and go so unprovided?

STANLEY.
You may jest on.

HASTINGS.
My lord, I hold my life as dear as you do yours;
Think you, but that I know our state secure,
I would be so triumphant as I am?

STANLEY.
>The lord at Pomfret, when he rode from London,
>Was jocund, and supposed his state was sure.
>Pray God, I say, I prove a needless coward!

HASTINGS.
>I tell thee, the world 'tis better with me now
>Than when I met thee last where now we meet:
>Then was I going prisoner to the Tower,
>By the suggestion of the Queen's brother;
>But now, I tell thee – keep it to thyself –
>This day that enemy is put to death,
>And I in better state than e'er I was.

RICHMOND.
>He, for his truth, might better wear his head
>Than some that have accused him wear their hats.

>*Exeunt.*

Scene Three

Enter GUARDS *carrying* RIVERS *to death.*

RIVERS.
>Now Margaret's curse is fall'n upon my head,
>Be satisfied, dear God, with my true blood,
>Which, as thou know'st, unjustly must be spilt.

>RIVERS *is killed.*

Scene Four

BUCKINGHAM, STANLEY, HASTINGS, BISHOP OF ELY
take their seats at a table.

HASTINGS.
My lords, at once: the cause why we are met
Is, to determine of the coronation.
In God's name, speak: when is the royal day?

BUCKINGHAM.
Is all things ready for that royal time?

STANLEY.
It is, and wants but nomination.

BISHOP OF ELY.
Tomorrow, then, I judge a happy day.

BUCKINGHAM.
Who knows the Lord Protector's mind herein?
Who is most inward with the noble Duke?

BISHOP OF ELY.
Your grace, we think, should soonest know his mind.

BUCKINGHAM.
We know each other's faces; for our hearts,
He knows no more of mine than I of yours;
Nor I of his, my lord, than you of mine.
Lord Hastings, you and he are near in love.

HASTINGS.
I thank his grace, I know he loves me well;
But, for his purpose in the coronation,
I have not sounded him, nor he deliver'd
His gracious pleasure any way therein:
But you, my noble lords, may name the time;
And in the Duke's behalf I'll give my voice,
Which, I presume, he'll take in gentle part.

Enter RICHARD, *with* CATESBY.

BUCKINGHAM.
Now in good time, here comes the Duke himself.

RICHARD.

My noble lords and cousins all, good morrow.
I have been long a sleeper; but, I hope,
My absence doth neglect no great design,
Which by my presence might have been concluded.

BUCKINGHAM.

Had not you come upon your cue, my lord
William Lord Hastings had pronounced your part, –
I mean, your voice, – for crowning of the King.

RICHARD.

Than my Lord Hastings no man might be bolder;
His lordship knows me well, and loves me well.

HASTINGS.

I thank your grace.

RICHARD.

Cousin of Buckingham, a word with you.

Drawing him aside.

Catesby hath sounded Hastings in our business,
And finds the testy gentleman so hot,
As he will lose his head ere give consent
His master's son, as worshipfully he terms it,
Shall lose the royalty of England's throne.

HASTINGS.

His grace looks cheerfully and smooth today;
There's some conceit or other likes him well,
When he doth bid good morrow with such spirit.
I think there's never a man in Christendom
That can less hide his love or hate than he,
For by his face straight shall you know his heart.

BISHOP OF ELY.

What of his heart perceive you in his face
By any likelihood he show'd today?

HASTINGS.

Marry, that with no man here he is offended;
For, were he, he had shown it in his looks.

STANLEY.
　I pray God he be not, I say.

　RICHARD *and* BUCKINGHAM, *advancing*.

RICHARD.
　I pray you all, tell me what they deserve
　That do conspire my death with devilish plots
　Of damned witchcraft, and that have prevail'd
　Upon my body with their hellish charms?

HASTINGS.
　The tender love I bear your grace, my lord,
　Makes me most forward in this noble presence
　To doom the offenders, whatsoever they be.
　I say, my lord, they have deserved death.

RICHARD.
　Then be your eyes the witness of their evil.
　See how I am bewitch'd; behold mine arm
　Is, like a blasted sapling, wither'd up;
　And this is Edward's wife, that monstrous witch,
　That by her witchcraft thus have marked me.

HASTINGS.
　If she hath done this deed, my noble lord –

RICHARD.
　If? Thou protector of this damned strumpet,
　Talk'st thou to me of 'ifs'? Thou art a traitor:
　Off with his head! Now, by St Paul I swear,
　I will not dine until I see the same.
　Catesby, look that it be done:
　The rest, that love me, rise and follow me.

　Exeunt all but HASTINGS *and* CATESBY *with* TYRREL.

HASTINGS.
　Woe, woe for England! Not a whit for me;
　For I, too fond, might have prevented this.
　Stanley did dream the boar did raze his helm;
　But I did scorn it and disdain to fly.

O Margaret, Margaret, now thy heavy curse
Is lighted on poor Hastings' wretched head!

CATESBY.

Dispatch, my lord; the Duke would break his fast.
Make a short shrift; he longs to see your head.

HASTINGS.

O momentary grace of mortal men,
Which we more hunt for than the grace of God!
Who builds his hopes in air of your good looks,
Lives like a drunken sailor on a mast,
Ready, with every nod, to tumble down
Into the fatal bowels of the deep.

CATESBY.

Come, come, dispatch; 'tis bootless to exclaim.

HASTINGS.

O bloody Richard! Miserable England!
I prophesy the fearful'st time to thee
That ever wretched age hath look'd upon.
Come, lead me to the block; bear him my head.
They smile at me who shortly shall be dead.

Exeunt.

Scene Five

Enter RICHARD *and* BUCKINGHAM, *with the* LORD
MAYOR.

BUCKINGHAM.

Well, well, he was the covert'st shelter'd traitor
That ever lived.
Would you imagine, or almost believe,
Were't not that by great preservation
We live to tell it you, the subtle traitor

This day had plotted, in the council house
To murder me and my good Lord of Gloucester?

LORD MAYOR.
What, had he so?

RICHARD.
What, think we would, against the form of law,
Proceed thus rashly to the villain's death,
But that the extreme peril of the case,
The peace of England, and our persons' safety,
Enforced us to this execution?

LORD MAYOR.
Now, fair befall you! He deserved his death;
And you my good lords, both have well proceeded,
To warn false traitors from the like attempts.
And doubt you not, right noble princes both,
But I'll acquaint our duteous citizens
With all your just proceedings in this cause.

RICHARD.
And to that end we wish'd your lordship here,
To avoid the carping censures of the world.

BUCKINGHAM.
And so, my Lord Mayor, adieu.

Exit LORD MAYOR.

RICHARD.
Go, after, after, cousin Buckingham.
The Mayor towards Guildhall hies him in all post.
Infer the bastardy of Edward's children:
Moreover, urge Edward's hateful lechery
And bestial appetite in change of lust;
Which stretched to their servants, daughters, wives,
Even where his lustful eye or savage heart,
Without control, listed to make his prey.

BUCKINGHAM.
Fear not, my lord, I'll play the orator
As if the golden fee for which I plead
Were for myself: and so, my lord, adieu.

Exit BUCKINGHAM.

Enter CATESBY *and* TYRREL *with* HASTINGS' *head,
and others.*

CATESBY.
    Here is the head of that ignoble traitor,
    The dangerous and unsuspected Hastings.

RICHARD.
    So dear I loved the man, that I must weep.
    I took him for the plainest harmless creature
    That breathed upon this earth a Christian.
    Made him my book wherein my soul recorded
    The history of all her secret thoughts:
    So smooth he daub'd his vice with show of virtue,
    That, his apparent open guilt omitted,
    He lived from all attainder of suspect.

MARGARET (*aside*).
    Here's a good world the while! Why who's so gross,
    That seeth not this palpable device?
    Yet who's so blind, but says he sees it not?
    Bad is the world; and all will come to nought,
    When such bad dealings must be seen in thought.

Enter BUCKINGHAM. *Exeunt all others.*

RICHARD.
    How now, my lord, what say the citizens?
    Touch'd you the bastardy of Edward's children?

BUCKINGHAM.
    I did; with the insatiate greed of his desires,
    His tyranny for trifles, his own bastardy,
    Your discipline in war, wisdom in peace,
    Your bounty, virtue, fair humility;
    And when mine oratory grew to an end
    I bid them that did love their country's good
    Cry 'God save Richard, England's royal King!'

RICHARD.
    And did they so?

BUCKINGHAM.
No. So God help me, they spake not a word.

RICHARD.
What tongueless blocks were they! Would not they speak?

CATESBY.
The Mayor is here at hand.

BUCKINGHAM.
Intend some fear;
Be not you spoke with, but by mighty suit;
And look you get a prayer book in your hand.
And be not easily won to our request:
Play the maid's part, still answer no, and take it.

RICHARD.
I go; and if you plead as well for them
As I can say nay to thee for myself,
No doubt we bring it to a happy issue.

Enter CATESBY.

CATESBY.
Go, go; the Lord Mayor comes.

Exit RICHARD *and* CATESBY.

Enter the LORD MAYOR *and* CITIZENS.

BUCKINGHAM.
Welcome, my lords; I dance attendance here;
I think the Duke will not be spoke withal.

Enter CATESBY.

Here comes his servant: how now, Catesby,
What says he?

CATESBY.
My lord: he doth entreat your grace
To visit him tomorrow or next day:
He is within, with two right reverend fathers,
Divinely bent to meditation.

BUCKINGHAM.
  Return, good Catesby, to the gracious Duke;
  Tell him myself, the Mayor and citizens,
  In deep designs and matters of great moment,
  No less importing than our general good,
  Are come to have some conference with his grace.

CATESBY.
  I'll signify so much unto him straight.

  Exit.

BUCKINGHAM.
  Ah, ha, my lord, this Prince is not an Edward!
  He is not lolling on a lewd love-bed,
  But on his knees at meditation;
  Not dallying with a brace of courtesans,
  But meditating with two deep divines;
  Not sleeping, to engross his idle body,
  But praying, to enrich his watchful soul.
  Happy were England, would this gracious Prince
  Take on himself the sovereignty thereof.
  But, sure, I fear, we shall ne'er win him to it.

LORD MAYOR.
  Marry, God forbid his grace should say us nay!

BUCKINGHAM.
  I fear he will.

  Re-enter CATESBY.

  How now, Catesby, what says your lord?

CATESBY.
  He wonders to what end you have assembled
  Such troops of citizens to speak with him.
  His grace not being warn'd thereof before:
  My lord, he fears you mean no good to him.

BUCKINGHAM.
  By Heaven, we come to him in perfect love!

  Enter RICHARD.

Famous Plantagenet, most gracious Prince,
Lend favourable ears to our request,
And pardon us the interruption
Of thy devotion and right Christian zeal.

RICHARD.
My lord, there needs no such apology.
I rather do beseech you pardon me,
Who, earnest in the service of my God,
Neglect the visitation of my friends.
I do suspect I have done some offence
That seems disgracious in the city's eyes,
And that you come to reprehend my ignorance.

BUCKINGHAM.
You have, my lord: would it might please your grace,
At our entreaties, to amend that fault!

RICHARD.
Else wherefore breathe I in a Christian land?

BUCKINGHAM.
Then know, it is your fault that you resign
The supreme seat, the throne majestical,
The scepter'd office of your ancestors,
Your state of fortune and your due of birth,
The lineal glory of your royal house,
To the corruption of a blemished stock;
Whilst, in the mildness of your sleepy thoughts,
Which here we waken to our country's good,
This noble isle doth want her proper limbs;
Her face defaced with scars of infamy,
Her royal stock graft with ignoble plants,
And almost shoulder'd in the swallowing gulf
Of blind forgetfulness and dark oblivion;
Which to recure, we heartily solicit
Your gracious self to take on you the charge
And kingly government of this your land,
Not as protector, steward, substitute,
Or lowly factor for another's gain;

But as successively from blood to blood,
Your right of birth, your empery, your own.

RICHARD.
Your love deserves my thanks; but my desert
Unmeritable shuns your high request.
Yet so much is my poverty of spirit,
So mighty and so many my defects,
That I had rather hide me from my greatness;
And, God be thank'd, there's no need of me:
The royal tree hath left us royal fruit,
Which, mellow'd by the stealing hours of time,
Will well become the seat of majesty,
And make, no doubt, us happy by his reign.

BUCKINGHAM.
My lord, this argues conscience in your grace,
But the respects thereof are nice and trivial,
All circumstances well considered.
You say that Edward is your brother's son:
So say we too, but to a care-crazed mother of many sons;
A beauty-waning and distressed widow,
Even in the afternoon of her best days,
Made prize and purchase of his lustful eye,
Seduced the pitch and height of all his thoughts
To base declension and loathed bigamy.
By her, in his unlawful bed, he got
This Edward, whom our manners call the Prince.
Then, good my lord, take to your royal self
This proffer'd benefit of dignity,
If not to bless us and the land withal,
Yet to draw forth your noble ancestry
From the corruption of abusing times
Unto a lineal true-derived course.

LORD MAYOR.
Do, good my lord. Your citizens entreat you.

BUCKINGHAM.
Refuse not, mighty lord, this proffer'd love.

CATESBY.

O, make them joyful, grant their lawful suit!

RICHARD.

Alas, why would you heap these cares on me?
I am unfit for state and majesty.
I do beseech you, take it not amiss;
I cannot nor I will not yield to you.

BUCKINGHAM.

Yet know, whe'er you accept our suit or no,
Your brother's son shall never reign our king,
But we will plant some other in the throne,
To the disgrace and downfall of your house:
And in this resolution here we leave you.
Come, citizens: zounds! I'll entreat no more.

RICHARD.

O, do not swear, my Lord of Buckingham.

Exit BUCKINGHAM *with some* CITIZENS.

CATESBY.

Call him again, sweet Prince, accept their suit.
If you deny them, all the land will rue it.

RICHARD.

Would you enforce me to a world of cares?
Well, call them again. I am not made of stone.
But penetrable to your kind entreaties,
Albeit against my conscience and my soul.

Re-enter BUCKINGHAM *and the rest*.

Cousin of Buckingham, and you sage, grave men,
Since you will buckle fortune on my back,
To bear her burden, whether I will or no,
I must have patience to endure the load.
But God He knows, and you may partly see,
How far I am from the desire thereof.

LORD MAYOR.

God bless your grace! We see it, and will say it.

RICHARD.
In saying so, you shall but say the truth.

BUCKINGHAM.
Then I salute you with this kingly title:
Long live Richard, England's worthy King!

LORD MAYOR *and* CITIZENS.
Long live Richard, England's worthy King!

STANLEY *and* RICHMOND, *with* BISHOP OF ELY.

STANLEY.
If thou wilt outstrip death, go cross the seas,
And live, dear Richmond, from the reach of Hell.
Go, hie thee, hie thee from this slaughterhouse.

Exeunt.

Interval.

ACT FOUR

Scene One

Enter KING RICHARD III, ANNE, BUCKINGHAM,
CATESBY, TYRREL, STANLEY, *and others*.

RICHARD.
Buckingham, thus high, by thy advice
And thy assistance, is King Richard seated.
But shall we wear these honours for a day?
Or shall they last, and we rejoice in them?

BUCKINGHAM.
Still live they and for ever may they last.

RICHARD.
O Buckingham, now do I play the touch,
To try if thou be current gold indeed:
Young Edward lives; think now what I would speak.

BUCKINGHAM.
Say on, my loving lord.

RICHARD.
Why, Buckingham, I say, I would be King.

BUCKINGHAM.
Why, so you are, my thrice-renowned liege.

RICHARD.
Ha! Am I King? 'Tis so – but Edward lives.

BUCKINGHAM.
True, noble Prince.

RICHARD.
                    O bitter consequence,
That Edward still should live: 'True, noble Prince!'
Cousin, thou wast not wont to be so dull.

Shall I be plain? I wish the bastards dead;
And I would have it suddenly perform'd.
What sayest thou? Speak suddenly. Be brief.

BUCKINGHAM.
Your grace may do your pleasure.

RICHARD.
Tut, tut, thou art all ice, thy kindness freezes.
Say, have I thy consent that they shall die?

BUCKINGHAM.
Give me some breath, some little pause, my lord,
Before I positively speak in this.
I will resolve you herein presently.

Exit.

RICHARD.
High-reaching Buckingham grows circumspect.
No more shall be the neighbour to my counsel:
Hath he so long held out with me, untired,
And stops he now for breath? Tyrrel?

TYRREL.
Your most obedient subject.

RICHARD.
                              Art thou, indeed?

TYRREL.
Prove me, my gracious sovereign.

RICHARD.
Dar'st thou resolve to kill a friend of mine?

TYRREL.
Ay, my lord; but I had rather kill two enemies.

RICHARD.
Why, there thou hast it: two deep enemies,
Foes to my rest and my sweet sleep's disturbers,
Are they that I would have thee deal upon.
Tyrrel, I mean those bastards in the Tower.

TYRREL.
Let me have open means to come to them,
And soon I'll rid you from the fear of them.

RICHARD.
Thou sing'st sweet music. Hark, come hither, Tyrrel.
Rise, and lend thine ear:

Whispers in his ear. Then:

There is no more but so: say it is done,
And I will love thee, and prefer thee too.

TYRREL.
I will dispatch it straight.

Exit.

RICHARD.
Catesby! What news with you?

CATESBY.
My lord, I hear that Richmond's fled.

RICHARD.
Stanley, he is your wife's son. Well, look to it.
Catesby!

CATESBY.
My lord?

RICHARD.
Rumour it abroad
That Anne, my wife, is very grievous sick.
I will take order for her keeping close.
Look, how thou dream'st! I say again, give out
That Anne my wife is sick and like to die.
About it, for it stands me much upon,
To stop all hopes whose growth may damage me.

Exit CATESBY.

Stanley! Look to your wife; if she convey
Letters to Richmond, you shall answer it.

Exit STANLEY.

I know that milksop Richmond aims
At young Elizabeth, my brother's daughter,
And, by that knot, looks proudly o'er the crown.
I must be married to my brother's daughter,
Or else my kingdom stands on brittle glass.

Re-enter BUCKINGHAM.

BUCKINGHAM.
My lord, I have consider'd in my mind
The late demand that you did sound me in.

RICHARD.
Well, let that pass. Richmond is fled.

BUCKINGHAM.
I hear that news, my lord.
My liege, I claim your gift, my due by promise,
For which your honour and your faith is pawn'd:
The earldom of Hereford and the moveables,
The which you have promised I shall possess.
What says Your Highness to my just demand?

RICHARD.
As I remember, Henry the Sixth
Did prophesy that Richmond should be king,
When Richmond was a little peevish boy.
A king. Perhaps, perhaps, –

BUCKINGHAM.
My lord!

RICHARD.
How chance the prophet could not at that time
Have told me, I being by, that I should kill him?

BUCKINGHAM.
My lord, your promise for the earldom, –

RICHARD.
Ay, what's o'clock?

BUCKINGHAM.
　I am thus bold to put your grace in mind
　Of what you promised me.

RICHARD.
　　　　　　　　　　　Well, but what's o'clock?

BUCKINGHAM.
　Upon the stroke of ten.

RICHARD.
　　　　　　　　　　　Well, let it strike.

BUCKINGHAM.
　Why let it strike?

RICHARD.
　Because that, like a jack, thou keep'st the stroke
　Betwixt thy begging and my meditation.
　I am not in the giving vein today.

　Exeunt all but BUCKINGHAM *and* ANNE.

BUCKINGHAM.
　And is it thus? Rewards he my true service
　With such deep contempt? Made I him King for this?

ANNE.
　When he that is my husband now came to me,
　When scarce the blood was well wash'd from his hands,
　Which issued from my other angel husband;
　O, when, I say, I look'd on Richard's face,
　This was my wish: 'Be thou,' quoth I, 'accursed,
　For making me, so young, so old a widow!
　And, when thou wed'st, let sorrow haunt thy bed;
　And be thy wife – if any be so mad –
　As miserable by the life of thee
　As thou hast made me by my dear lord's death!'
　Lo, I proved the subject of my own soul's curse,
　Which ever since hath kept my eyes from rest;
　For never yet one hour in his bed
　Have I enjoy'd the golden dew of sleep,
　But have been waked by his timorous dreams.

Besides, he hates me;
And will, no doubt, shortly be rid of me.

BUCKINGHAM.
Poor heart, adieu! O, let me think on Hastings
And be gone, and swiftly while my fearful head is on.

Exit.

ANNE *is murdered.*

Scene Two

Enter TYRREL.

TYRREL.
The tyrannous and bloody deed is done.
The most arch of piteous massacre
That ever yet this land was guilty of.

Enter RICHARD.

RICHARD.
Kind Tyrrel, am I happy in thy news?

TYRREL.
If to have done the thing you gave in charge
Beget your happiness, be happy then,
For it is done.

RICHARD.
But didst thou see them dead?

TYRREL.
I did, my lord.

RICHARD.
                    And buried, gentle Tyrrel?

TYRREL.
The chaplain of the Tower hath buried them,
But where, to say the truth, I do not know.

RICHARD.

  Come to me, Tyrrel, soon at after-supper,
  And thou shalt tell the process of their death.
  Meantime, but think how I may do thee good,
  And be inheritor of thy desire.
  Farewell till then.

  Exit TYRREL.

  The sons of Edward sleep in Abraham's bosom,
  And Anne my wife hath bid this world goodnight.
  To my brother's daughter I go, a jolly thriving wooer.
  Murder her brothers, and then marry her! –
  Uncertain way of gain. But I am in
  So far in blood that sin will pluck on sin.
  Tear-falling pity dwells not in this eye.

  Enter CATESBY.

CATESBY.

  Bad news, my lord: Ely is fled to Richmond,
  And Buckingham, back'd with the hardy Welshmen,
  Is in the field, and still his power increaseth.

RICHARD.

  Ely with Richmond troubles me more near
  Than Buckingham and his rash-levied army.
  Go, muster men. My counsel is my shield.
  We must be brief when traitors brave the field.

  Exeunt.

Scene Three

Enter ELIZABETH *and the* DUCHESS OF YORK.

ELIZABETH.
Ah, my young Princes! Ah, my tender babes!
If yet your gentle souls fly in the air
Hover about me with your airy wings
And hear your mother's lamentation.

DUCHESS OF YORK.
So many miseries have crazed my voice,
That my woe-wearied tongue is mute and dumb.

Enter MARGARET.

MARGARET.
Richard yet lives, Hell's black intelligencer.
Earth gapes, Hell burns, fiends roar, saints pray
To have him suddenly convey'd away.
Cancel his bond of life, dear God, I pray,
That I may live to say, 'the dog is dead!'

ELIZABETH.
O, thou didst prophesy the time would come
That I should wish for thee to help me curse
That bottled spider, that foul bunch-back'd toad.
O thou well skill'd in curses, stay awhile,
And teach me how to curse mine enemies!

MARGARET.
Where is thy husband now? Where be thy brother?
Where are thy children? Wherein dost thou joy?
Who sues to thee and cries 'God save the Queen'?
Where be the bending peers that flatter'd thee?
Where be the thronging troops that follow'd thee?
Decline all this, and see what now thou art:
For happy wife, a most distressed widow;
For joyful mother, one that wails the name;
For one that scorn'd at me, now scorn'd of me;
For one being fear'd of all, now fearing one;
For one commanding all, obey'd of none.

Thus hath the course of justice wheel'd about,
And left thee but a very prey to time.
Thou didst usurp my place, and dost thou not
Usurp the just proportion of my sorrow?

ELIZABETH.
My words are dull; O, quicken them with thine!

MARGARET.
Thy woes will make them sharp, and pierce like mine.

Exit MARGARET.

Enter RICHARD, *with* CATESBY *and* TYRREL.

ELIZABETH.
Tell me, thou villain slave, where are my children?

DUCHESS OF YORK.
Thou toad, thou toad, where is thy brother Clarence?

RICHARD.
Who intercepts my expedition?

DUCHESS OF YORK.
O, she that might have intercepted thee,
By strangling thee in her accursed womb
From all the slaughters, wretch, that thou hast done!

RICHARD.
A flourish, trumpets! Strike alarum, drums!
Let not the heavens hear these tell-tale women
Rail on the Lord's anointed: strike, I say!

Drums and trumpets. Alarums.

Either be patient and entreat me fair,
Or with the clamorous report of war
Thus will I drown your exclamations.

DUCHESS OF YORK.
Art thou my son?

RICHARD.
Ay, I thank God, my father, and yourself.

DUCHESS OF YORK.
  Then patiently hear my impatience.

RICHARD.
  Madam, I have a touch of your condition,
  Which cannot brook the accent of reproof.

DUCHESS OF YORK.
  O, let me speak!

RICHARD.
                    Do then: but I'll not hear.

DUCHESS OF YORK.
  I will be mild and gentle in my speech.

RICHARD.
  And brief, good Mother; for I am in haste.

DUCHESS OF YORK.
  Art thou so hasty? I have stay'd for thee,
  God knows, in torment and in agony.

RICHARD.
  And came I not at last to comfort you?

DUCHESS OF YORK.
  No, by the Holy Rood, thou know'st it well:
  Thou cam'st on Earth to make the Earth my Hell.
  A grievous burden was thy birth to me;
  Tetchy and wayward was thy infancy;
  Thy school days frightful, desperate, wild, and furious,
  Thy prime of manhood daring, bold, and venturous,
  Thy age confirm'd, proud, subtle, sly and bloody,
  More mild, but yet more harmful, kind in hatred.
  What comfortable hour canst thou name,
  That ever graced me with thy company?

RICHARD.
  If I be so disgracious in your sight,
  Let me march on, and not offend you, madam.
  Strike the drum.

DUCHESS OF YORK.
>   I prithee, hear me speak.

RICHARD.
    You speak too bitterly.

DUCHESS OF YORK.
>   Hear me a word,
    For I shall never speak to thee again.

RICHARD.
    So.

DUCHESS OF YORK.
    Either thou wilt die, by God's just ordinance,
    Ere from this war thou turn a conqueror,
    Or I with grief and age shall perish
    And never look upon thy face again.
    Therefore take with thee my most heavy curse,
    Which, in the day of battle, tire thee more
    Than all the complete armour that thou wear'st.
    My prayers on the adverse party fight,
    And there the little souls of Edward's children
    Whisper the spirits of thine enemies
    And promise them success and victory.
    Bloody thou art, bloody will be thy end;
    Shame serves thy life and doth thy death attend.

    Exit.

ELIZABETH.
    Though far more cause, yet much less spirit to curse
    Abides in me; I say amen to all.

RICHARD.
    Stay, madam; I must speak a word with you.

ELIZABETH.
    I have no more sons of the royal blood
    For thee to murder.

RICHARD.
>   You have a daughter.
    Virtuous and fair, royal and gracious.

ELIZABETH.

And must she die for this? O, let her live,
And I'll corrupt her manners, stain her beauty;
So she may live unscarr'd of bleeding slaughter,
I will confess she was not Edward's daughter.

RICHARD.

Wrong not her birth, she is of royal blood.

ELIZABETH.

To save her life, I'll say she is not so.

RICHARD.

Her life is only safest in her birth.

ELIZABETH.

And only in that safety died her brothers.

RICHARD.

You speak as if that I had slain the Princes.

ELIZABETH.

No doubt the murderous knife was dull and blunt
Till it was whetted on thy stone-hard heart,
To revel in the entrails of my lambs.

RICHARD.

Madam, so thrive I in my enterprise
And dangerous success of bloody wars,
As I intend more good to you and yours
Than ever you or yours by me were harmed!

ELIZABETH.

Tell me what state, what dignity, what honour,
Canst thou demise to any child of mine?

RICHARD.

Even all I have – ay, and myself and all –
Will I withal endow a child of thine.

ELIZABETH.

Be brief, lest that the process of thy kindness
Last longer telling than thy kindness' date.

RICHARD.
Then know, that from my soul I love thy daughter.
And mean to make her Queen of England.

ELIZABETH.
Say then, who dost thou mean shall be her King?

RICHARD.
Even he that makes her Queen. Who else should be?

ELIZABETH.
What, thou?

RICHARD.
I, even I: what think you of it?

ELIZABETH.
How canst thou woo her?

RICHARD.
That would I learn of you,
As one being best acquainted with her humour.

ELIZABETH.
And wilt thou learn of me?

RICHARD.
Madam, with all my heart.

ELIZABETH.
Send to her, by the man that slew her brothers,
A pair of bleeding hearts; thereon engrave
'Edward' and 'York'; then haply she will weep.
Therefore present to her
A handkerchief; which, say to her, did drain
The purple sap from her sweet brother's body,
And bid her dry her weeping eyes therewith.
If this inducement move her not to love,
Send her a story of thy noble acts;
Tell her thou mad'st away her Uncle Clarence,
Her Uncle Rivers; yea, and, for her sake,
Mad'st quick conveyance with her good aunt Anne.

RICHARD.
Come, come, you mock me; this is not the way
To win your daughter.

ELIZABETH.
There is no other way,
Unless thou couldst put on some other shape,
And not be Richard, that hath done all this.

RICHARD.
Say that I did all this for love of her.

ELIZABETH.
Nay, then indeed she cannot choose but hate thee,
Having bought love with such a bloody spoil.

RICHARD.
Look, what is done cannot be now amended.
Men shall deal unadvisedly sometimes,
Which after hours give leisure to repent.
If I did take the kingdom from your sons,
To make amends, I'll give it to your daughter.
The loss you have is but a son being king,
And by that loss your daughter is made queen.
I cannot make you what amends I would,
Therefore accept such kindness as I can.
What! we have many goodly days to see.
The liquid drops of tears that you have shed
Shall come again, transform'd to orient pearl,
Advantaging their loan with interest
Of ten times double gain of happiness.
Go, then my mother, to thy daughter go.
Make bold her bashful years with your experience;
Prepare her ears to hear a wooer's tale;
Put in her tender heart th'aspiring flame
Of golden sovereignty; acquaint the Princess
With the sweet silent hours of marriage joys;
And when this arm of mine hath chastised
The petty rebel, dull-brain'd Buckingham,
Bound with triumphant garlands will I come
And lead thy daughter to a conqueror's bed;

To whom I will retail my conquest won,
And she shall be sole victress, Caesar's Caesar.

ELIZABETH.
What were I best to say? Her father's brother
Would be her lord? Or shall I say her uncle?
Or, he that slew her brothers and her uncles?
Under what title shall I woo for thee?

RICHARD.
Say that the King, that may command, entreats.

ELIZABETH.
That at her hands which the King's King forbids.

RICHARD.
Say, I will love her everlastingly.

ELIZABETH.
But how long shall that title 'ever' last?

RICHARD.
Sweetly in force, unto her fair life's end.

ELIZABETH.
But how long fairly shall her sweet life last?

RICHARD.
So long as Heaven and nature lengthens it.

ELIZABETH.
So long as Hell and Richard likes of it.

RICHARD.
Your reasons are too shallow and too quick.

ELIZABETH.
O no, my reasons are too deep and dead;
Too deep and dead, poor infants, in their grave.

RICHARD.
Harp not on that string, madam; that is past.

ELIZABETH.
Harp on it still shall I, till heart-strings break.

RICHARD.

In her consists my happiness and thine;
Without her, follows to this land and me,
To thee, herself, and many a Christian soul,
Death, desolation, ruin and decay.
It cannot be avoided but by this;
It will not be avoided but by this.
Therefore, good Mother, – I must call you so –
Be the attorney of my love to her:
Plead what I will be, not what I have been;
Urge the necessity and state of times.

ELIZABETH.

Shall I be tempted of the Devil thus?

RICHARD.

Ay, if the Devil tempt thee to do good.

ELIZABETH.

Shall I forget myself to be myself?

RICHARD.

Ay, if yourself's remembrance wrong yourself.

ELIZABETH.

Yet thou didst kill my children.

RICHARD.

But in your daughter's womb I bury them:
Where in that nest of spicery they shall breed
Selves of themselves, to your recomforture.

ELIZABETH.

Shall I go win my daughter to thy will?

RICHARD.

And be a happy mother by the deed.

ELIZABETH.

I go. Write to me very shortly.
And you shall understand from me her mind.

RICHARD.

Bear her my true love's kiss; and so, farewell.

Exit ELIZABETH.

Relenting fool, and shallow, changing woman!
How now! What news?

TYRREL.
My gracious sovereign, on the western coast
Rideth a puissant navy to our shores.
'Tis thought that Richmond is their admiral;
And there they hull, expecting but the aid
Of Buckingham to welcome them ashore.

RICHARD.
Some light-foot friend post to the Duke of Norfolk:
Tyrrel, thyself, or Catesby; where is he?

CATESBY.
Here, my lord.

RICHARD.
                    Fly to the Duke.

(*To* TYRREL.)   Post thou to Salisbury.
When thou comest thither –

(*To* CATESBY.)   Dull, unmindful villain,
Why stand'st thou still, and go'st not to the Duke?

CATESBY.
First, mighty sovereign, let me know your mind,
What from your grace I shall deliver to him.

RICHARD.
O, true, good Catesby: bid him levy straight
The greatest strength and power he can make.

CATESBY.
I go.

Exit.

TYRREL.
What is't Your Highness' pleasure I shall do at Salisbury?

RICHARD.
Why, what wouldst thou do there before I go?

TYRREL.
Your Highness told me I should post before.

RICHARD.
My mind is changed, sir, my mind is changed.

Exit TYRREL.

Enter STANLEY.

How now, what news with you?

STANLEY.
None good, my lord, to please you with the hearing;
Nor none so bad, but may well be reported.

RICHARD.
Hoyday, a riddle! Neither good nor bad!
Why dost thou run so many miles about,
When thou mayst tell thy tale a nearer way?
Once more, what news?

STANLEY.
Richmond is on the seas.

RICHARD.
There let him sink, and be the seas on him!
White-liver'd runagate, what doth he there?

STANLEY.
I know not, mighty sovereign, but by guess.

RICHARD.
Well, sir, as you guess, as you guess?

STANLEY.
Stirr'd up by Buckingham, and Ely,
He makes for England, there to claim the crown.

RICHARD.
Is the chair empty? Is the sword unsway'd?
Is the King dead? The empire unpossess'd?
What heir of York is there alive but we?
And who is England's king but great York's heir?
Then, tell me, what doth he upon the seas?

STANLEY.

Unless for that, my liege, I cannot guess.

RICHARD.

Unless for that he comes to be your liege,
You cannot guess wherefore he comes.
Thou wilt revolt, and fly to him, I fear.

STANLEY.

No, mighty liege; therefore mistrust me not.

RICHARD.

Where is thy power, then, to beat him back?
Where be thy tenants and thy followers?
Are they not now upon the western shore?
Safe-conducting the rebels from their ships!

STANLEY.

They have not been commanded, mighty King.
Pleaseth Your Majesty to give me leave,
I'll muster up my friends, and meet your grace
Where and what time Your Majesty shall please.

RICHARD.

Ay, ay, thou wouldst be gone to join with Richmond.
I will not trust you, sir.

STANLEY.

                              Most mighty sovereign,
You have no cause to hold my friendship doubtful:
I never was, nor never will be, false.

RICHARD.

Well, go muster men; but, hear you, leave behind
Your son, George Stanley. Look your heart be firm,
Or else his head's assurance is but frail.

STANLEY.

So deal with him as I prove true to you.

Exit STANLEY.

Enter TYRREL.

TYRREL.
My lord, the army of the Duke of Buckingham –

RICHARD.
Out on you, owls! Nothing but songs of death?

He strikes him.

Take that, until thou bring me better news.

TYRREL.
The news I have to tell Your Majesty
Is, that by sudden floods and fall of waters,
Buckingham's army is dispersed and scatter'd;
And he himself wander'd away alone,
No man knows whither.

RICHARD.
                                        I cry thee mercy.

Enter CATESBY.

CATESBY.
My liege, the Duke of Buckingham is taken.
That is the best news. That the Earl of Richmond
Is with a mighty power landed at Milford,
Is colder tidings, yet they must be told.

RICHARD.
A royal battle might be won and lost!
Someone take order Buckingham be brought;
The rest march on with me.

Exeunt.

Scene Four

Enter LORD STANLEY.

STANLEY.
    Tell Richmond this from me:
    Tell him the Queen hath heartily consented
    Richmond shall espouse Elizabeth her daughter.
    But in the sty of this most bloody boar,
    My son George Stanley is frank'd up in hold.
    If I revolt, off goes young George's head;
    The fear of that withholds my present aid.
    Farewell.

    Exit.

ACT FIVE

Scene One

Enter CATESBY *with* BUCKINGHAM, *led to execution.*

BUCKINGHAM.
Will not King Richard let me speak with him?

CATESBY.
No, my good lord; therefore be patient.

BUCKINGHAM.
This is All Souls' Day, Catesby, is it not?

CATESBY.
It is, my lord.

BUCKINGHAM.
Why, then All Souls' Day is my body's doomsday.
This is the day that, in King Edward's time,
I wish't might fall on me when I was found
False to his children or his wife's allies.
This is the day wherein I wish'd to fall
By the false faith of him whom most I trusted.
That high All-Seer that I dallied with
Hath turn'd my feigned prayer on my head
And given in earnest what I begg'd in jest.
Thus doth he force the swords of wicked men
To turn their own points on their masters' bosoms.
Now Margaret's curse falls heavy on my neck:

With MARGARET.

'When he,' quoth she, 'shall split thy heart with sorrow,
Remember Margaret was a prophetess.'
Come, sir, convey me to the block of shame;
Wrong hath but wrong, and blame the due of blame.

CATESBY *murders* BUCKINGHAM.

Exeunt.

Scene Two

Enter RICHMOND *and others*.

RICHMOND.
Fellows in arms, and my most loving friends,
Bruised underneath the yoke of tyranny,
Thus far into the bowels of the land
Have we march'd on without impediment.
The weary sun hath made a golden set,
And by the bright track of his fiery car,
Gives signal, of a goodly day tomorrow.
Give me some ink and paper.
I'll draw the form and model of our battle,
Limit each leader to his several charge,
And part in just proportion our small strength.

Enter, on the other side, RICHARD *in arms*, CATESBY *and*
TYRELL.

RICHARD.
Here will I lie tonight;
But where tomorrow? Well, all's one for that.

Enter DUKE OF NORFOLK.

My Lord of Norfolk.

NORFOLK.
Here, most gracious liege.

RICHARD.
Norfolk, we must have knocks, ha, must we not?

NORFOLK.
We must both give and take, my loving lord.

RICHARD.
Who hath descried the number of the traitors?

NORFOLK.
Six or seven thousand is their utmost power.

RICHARD.
Well, the King's name is a tower of strength
Which they upon the adverse faction want.
Tyrell, what is't o'clock?

TYRREL.
It's supper-time, my lord; it's nine o'clock.

RICHARD.
I will not sup tonight. Give me some ink and paper.
Send out a pursuivant at arms
To Stanley's regiment; bid him bring his power
Before sun-rising, lest his son George fall
Into the blind cave of eternal night.
Fill me a bowl of wine.
I have not that alacrity of spirit,
Nor cheer of mind, that I was wont to have.
Bid my guard watch. Leave me.
About the mid of night come and help to arm me.
Leave me, I say.

Exit NORFOLK, CATESBY *and* TYRREL. RICHARD
sleeps.

Enter STANLEY *to* RICHMOND, *others attending*
RICHMOND.

RICHMOND.
All comfort that the dark night can afford
Be to thy person, noble Stanley!

STANLEY.
Fortune and victory sit on thy helm!
In brief, – for so the season bids us be, –
Prepare thy battle early in the morning.
I, as I may – that which I would, I cannot, –
With best advantage will deceive the time,

And aid thee in this doubtful shock of arms.
Farewell. The leisure and the fearful time
Cuts off the ceremonious vows of love
And ample interchange of sweet discours,
Which so-long-sunder'd friends should dwell upon.
God give us leisure for these rites of love.
Once more, adieu: be valiant, and speed well!

RICHMOND.
Good friends, conduct him to his regiment:
I'll strive, with troubled thoughts, to take a nap,
Lest leaden slumber peise me down tomorrow,
When I should mount with wings of victory:
Once more, goodnight, kind friends and gentlemen.

Exeunt all but RICHMOND.

O Thou, whose captain I account myself,
Look on my forces with a gracious eye;
Make us Thy ministers of chastisement,
That we may praise Thee in the victory!
To Thee I do commend my watchful soul,
Ere I let fall the windows of mine eyes:
Sleeping and waking, O, defend me still!

Sleeps.

Enter the GHOST OF ANNE.

GHOST OF ANNE (*to* RICHARD).
Richard, thy wife, that wretched Anne, thy wife,
That never slept a quiet hour with thee,
Now fills thy sleep with perturbations.
Tomorrow in the battle think on me,
And fall thy edgeless sword: despair, and die!

Enter the GHOSTS OF THE TWO YOUNG PRINCES.

GHOSTS OF YOUNG PRINCES (*to* RICHARD).
Think on thy nephews smother'd in the Tower:
Let us be lead within thy bosom, Richard,
And weigh thee down to ruin, shame, and death!
(*To* RICHMOND.) Sleep, Richmond, sleep in peace and
   wake in joy.

GHOST OF ANNE (*to* RICHMOND).
> Dream of success and happy victory.
> Thy adversary's wife doth pray for thee.

GHOSTS OF YOUNG PRINCES.
> Thy nephews' souls bid thee (*With* ANNE.) despair and die!

The GHOSTS *vanish.*

RICHARD *starts out of his dream.*

RICHARD.
> Have mercy, Jesu! – Soft! I did but dream.
> O coward conscience, how dost thou afflict me!
> Cold fearful drops stand on my trembling flesh.
> What do I fear? Myself? There's none else by:
> Richard loves Richard, that is, I and I.
> Is there a murderer here? No. Yes, I am.
> Then fly! What, from myself? Great reason why?
> Lest I revenge. What, myself upon myself?
> Alack. I love myself. Wherefore? For any good
> That I myself have done unto myself?
> O, no. Alas, I rather hate myself
> For hateful deeds committed by myself!
> I am a villain. Yet I lie; I am not.
> Fool, of thyself speak well. Fool, do not flatter.
> My conscience hath a thousand several tongues,
> And every tongue brings in a several tale,
> And every tale condemns me for a villain.
> All several sins, all used in each degree,
> Throng to the bar, crying all, 'Guilty! Guilty!'
> I shall despair. There is no creature loves me.
> And if I die, no soul shall pity me.
> And wherefore should they, since that I myself
> Find in myself no pity to myself?

Enter CATESBY.

CATESBY.
> My lord!

RICHARD.
> Zounds! who is there?

CATESBY.
Your friends are up, and buckle on their armour.

RICHARD.
O Catesby, I have dream'd a fearful dream!
What think'st thou, will our friends prove all true?

CATESBY.
No doubt, my lord.

RICHARD.
O Catesby, I fear, I fear, –

CATESBY.
Nay, good my lord, be not afraid of shadows.

Enter the LORDS *to* RICHMOND.

RICHMOND.
Cry mercy, lords and watchful gentlemen,
That you have ta'en a tardy sluggard here.

LORD.
How have you slept, my lord?

RICHMOND.
The sweetest sleep, and fairest-boding dreams
That ever enter'd in a drowsy head
Have I since your departure had, my lords.

RICHARD.
Who saw the sun today?

CATESBY.
Not I, my lord.

RICHARD.
Then he disdains to shine; for by the book
He should have braved the east an hour ago.
A black day will it be to somebody.

RICHMOND.
More than I have said, loving countrymen,
The leisure and enforcement of the time

Forbids to dwell upon. Yet remember this:
God and our good cause fight upon our side.

RICHARD.
Go, gentlemen, every man unto his charge.
Let not our babbling dreams affright our souls.
Conscience is but a word that cowards use,
Devised at first to keep the strong in awe.
Our strong arms be our conscience, swords our law.

RICHMOND.
Those whom we fight against
Had rather have us win than him they follow.
For what is he they follow? Truly, gentlemen,
A bloody tyrant and a homicide;
One raised in blood, and one in blood establish'd.

RICHARD.
What shall I say more than I have inferr'd?
Remember whom you are to cope withal:
A sort of vagabonds, rascals, and runaways,
A scum of beggars, and base lackey peasants,
Whom their o'er-cloyed country vomits forth
To desperate ventures and assured destruction.

RICHMOND.
If you do sweat to put a tyrant down,
You sleep in peace, the tyrant being slain;
If you do fight against your country's foes,
Your country's fat shall pay your pains the hire.
If you do fight in safeguard of your wives,
Your wives shall welcome home the conquerors.
If you do free your children from the sword,
Your children's children quit it in your age.

RICHARD.
You sleeping safe, they bring to you unrest;
You having lands, and blest with beauteous wives,
They would restrain the one, distain the other.
Shall these enjoy our lands? Lie with our wives?
Ravish our daughters?

RICHMOND.
> For me, the ransom of my bold attempt
> Shall be this cold corpse on the earth's cold face;
> But if I thrive, the gain of my attempt
> The least of you shall share his part thereof.
> God, and St George, Richmond, and victory!

RICHARD.
> What says Lord Stanley? Will he bring his power?

TYRREL.
> My lord, he doth deny to come.

RICHARD.
> Off with his son George's head!

TYRREL.
> After the battle let George Stanley die.

RICHARD.
> A thousand hearts are great within my bosom:
> March on, join bravely, let us to't pell-mell;
> If not to Heaven, then hand in hand to Hell.

Exeunt. Battle.

Enter the GHOST OF CLARENCE.

GHOST OF CLARENCE (*to* RICHARD).
> Let me sit heavy on thy soul!
> Poor Clarence, by thy guile betrayed to death!
> Fall thy edgeless sword: despair, and die! –

Enter the GHOST OF RIVERS.

GHOST OF RIVERS (*to* RICHARD).
> Let me sit heavy on thy soul,
> Rivers that died at Pomfret! Despair, and die!

Enter the GHOST OF HASTINGS.

GHOST OF HASTINGS (*to* RICHARD).
> Bloody and guilty, guiltily awake,
> And in a bloody battle end thy days!
> Think on Lord Hastings: despair, and die!

Enter the GHOST OF BUCKINGHAM.

GHOST OF BUCKINGHAM (*to* RICHARD).
  The first was I that helped thee to the crown;
  The last was I that felt thy tyranny.
  O, bloody Richard, think on Buckingham
  And die in terror of thy guiltiness!
  Think on, think on, of bloody deeds and death:
  Fainting, despair; despairing, yield thy breath!

Exeunt.

Scene Three

Alarum: excursions. CATESBY *to* TYRREL.

CATESBY.
  The King enacts more wonders than a man,
  Daring an opposite to every danger,
  Seeking for Richmond in the throat of death.
  Rescue, rescue, or else the day is lost!

CATESBY *is killed.*

Alarums. Enter RICHARD.

TYRREL.
  Withdraw, my lord; we'll help you to escape.

RICHARD.
  Slave, I have set my life upon a cast,
  And I will stand the hazard of the die.

TYRREL *are* NORFOLK *are killed.*

  I think there be six Richmonds in the field;
  Five have I slain today instead of him.

Enter RICHMOND.

  A horse, a horse! My kingdom for a horse!

They fight. RICHARD *is slain*.

RICHMOND.
God and your arms be praised, victorious friends:
The day is ours, the bloody dog is dead.

STANLEY.
Courageous Richmond, well hast thou acquit thee.

RICHMOND.
But, tell me, is young George Stanley living?

STANLEY.
He is, my lord, and safe.

RICHMOND.
England hath long been mad, and scarr'd herself;
The brother blindly shed the brother's blood;
The father rashly slaughter'd his own son;
The son, compell'd, been butcher to the sire.
All this divided York and Lancaster,
Divided in their dire division.
O, now, let Richmond and young Elizabeth,
The true succeeders of each royal house,
By God's fair ordinance conjoin together!
And let their heirs, God, if Thy will be so,
Enrich the time to come with smooth-faced peace,
With smiling plenty and fair prosperous days!
Abate the edge of traitors, gracious Lord,
That would reduce these bloody days again
And make poor England weep in streams of blood.
Let them not live to taste this land's increase
That would with treason wound this fair land's peace.
Now civil wounds are stopp'd; peace lives again.
That she may long live here, God say amen!

Exeunt.

End.

www.nickhernbooks.co.uk

facebook.com/nickhernbooks

twitter.com/nickhernbooks